Writers on Writing

GUIDE TO WRITING AND ILLUSTRATING CHILDREN'S BOOKS

Edited by
DAVID BOOTH

OVERLEA
HOUSE

Published by
OVERLEA HOUSE
20 Torbay Road
Markham, Ontario
L3R 1G6

1234567890   ML   7654321098

Canadian Cataloguing in Publication Data

Main entry under title:

Writers on writing

ISBN 0-7172-2393-0

1. Children's literature—Technique.
2. Authorship.   3. Authors and publishers.
I. Booth, David.

PN147.5.W75 1989   808.06'8   C89-094605-9

Table of Contents

Introduction
David Booth

Children's Picture-Books
Ian Wallace   *The Emotional Link*   9
Laszlo Gal   *Illustrating the Text*   12
Ted Harrison   *Images of the North*   16
Stéphane Poulin   *L'Illustration pour enfants/ Illustrating for Children*   20

Writing for the Beginning Reader
Susan Wallace   *Writing Easy-Reads for Juvenile Readers*   29
Maryann Kovalski   *Patterns and Structures for Writing*   36
Ted Staunton   *Inviting the Reader into the Story*   40

Writing for Juveniles
Jean Little   *How I Do It*   46
Bernice Thurman Hunter   *Getting Started*   52
Ken Roberts   *Writing Humorous Stories*   56
Eric Wilson   *Developing a Series*   59
Marion Crook   *Writing Mystery Stories*   62
Jean Booker   *Writing Short Stories*   67
Meguido Zola   *Non-Fiction: Biographies*   71

Writing for Young Adults
Janet Lunn   *The Joy of Writing*   77
Claire Mackay   *What's in a Name: Selecting Names for Your Characters*   82
Barbara Smucker   *Historical Fiction*   88
Monica Hughes   *Writing Science Fiction and Fantasy*   91

Writing Poetry for Children

sean o huigin   *Narrative Poetry*   96

Diane Dawber   *Poems with Children in Mind*   100

Mary Blakeslee   *Bubble Gum and Birthdays*   106

Filling Special Needs

Eva Martin   *New Stories from Old*   112

Celia Barker Lottridge   *Folktales as a Source for Writing*   116

Beatrice Culleton   *Native Peoples*   120

David Dueck   *Film Writing*   124

Sylvia Funston   *Writing for Children's Magazines*   127

William H. Moore   *Writing for Textbooks*   131

Publishing Books for Children

Valerie Hussey   *The Role of the Publisher*   137

Stanley Skinner   *The Editor*   143

Joanne Kellock   *The Role of the Agent*   149

Bringing Books to Children

Kathy Lowinger   *Blowing Your Horn: The Author as Promoter*   156

Joan McGrath   *Reviewing Books for Children*   160

Tim Wynne-Jones   *To Pass On the Good News: Reviewing Books for Children*   164

Marge Kelley   *The Role of the Library*   169

Judy Sarick   *The Role of the Bookstore*   173

Biographies   *177*

Bibliography   *190*

Biographies   177

Bibliography   190

Introduction

David Booth

Because of my involvement with children's books in education, each year I am asked the same question by many different people: "How do you get a book for children published?" Children's literature has become a popular art form; even members of royalty are now writing storybooks. Perhaps they are trying to recapture childhood, or to hold it to a golden light; maybe the simplicity of the form beckons them as beginning authors; it could be that they want to entertain or inform children with a story hidden in their imaginations. However, writing for children is an art form, and for a book to be successful, the author must recognize the difficulties and problems involved, and set about the task as professionally as possible. Children are a special audience, deserving of respect and needful of quality in the books they listen to and read. Authors who wish to reach children must begin by understanding them, learning about their interests and feelings, exploring the many styles and formats used in publishing, and finding ways to breathe life into their ideas.

The last decade in Canada has seen tremendous growth of book publishing for young audiences. At the same time, Canada has become the largest book-importing country in the world, with imports from America and Great Britain filling our bookshelves. Books for children are a big industry. Parents are realizing the importance of literature in the lives of their children; schools are using "real books" as the basis of the language arts curriculum; children's bookstores have appeared throughout the country; there are journals and newspaper columns devoted to the criticism of children's books; awards and promotion agencies are heightening public awareness, and Canadian authors and illustrators are being recognized and respected for the quality of their work. As well, Canadian books are now found in other countries, translated into other languages. Still, very few publishing houses in Canada produce children's books, and the market for new authors is limited and difficult to break into. However, the public is beginning to recognize the value of children's books, and the next few years will be strong ones for publishing in this field. It is a good time for prospective authors of books for children, and it has been a long time in coming.

Before writing a book, you will have to face some vital questions:

- Will you write for a pre-school, primary, juvenile or young adult audience?

- Will you work in non-fiction, fiction or poetry?
- Will you write picture-books, easy-read books, juvenile novels or young adult fiction?
- Will you write books, short stories, magazine articles, or work in specialized areas such as film or television scripts?

It will take writing and more writing for you to hone your skills. At the same time, you can work your way through the collection at the children's library, read your work aloud to children, talk to them about what does and doesn't work, listen to publishers and editors, and talk to other writers for children at book fairs and at schools. You must be professional in your approach to becoming a children's writer.

The articles in this book have been written by those who both create for and bring books to this special, select audience. The authors are speaking directly to you, sharing the information and advice they have accumulated on their journeys to published success, building a general perspective of writing for a young audience. We cannot cover the entire world of publishing for children in one book, so we have attempted to provide personal overviews that include instructions and opportunities for helping aspiring writers to begin. You will find articles by authors, illustrators, poets, editors, publishers, librarians, critics and advocates of books for children. Each article has been selected to help create for you a wide picture of the world of publishing for young audiences. Putting your ideas down is first and foremost, but getting a book published involves more than that. It is my hope that this book will help you in your understanding of the process, and strengthen your will to publish for children.

David Booth

1

Children's Picture-Books

Introduction

For young children, the picture-book is a lifeline to literacy and learning. As well, it is an experience of closeness, bringing the reader and the child together in a mutually satisfying relationship. Parents introduce children to the reading habit with a picture-book before bed; teachers know the power of story and response in their classrooms and use picture-books for shared literary activities and for encouraging further follow-ups through storytelling, painting and drama. In many schools now, older children are reading to younger children and everyone benefits from this powerful medium. Children feel comfortable with picture-books because the visual information is accessible to them, and the story and the language that the adult is bringing to life complement the visuals so that the potential for meaning-making is strong. The children are drawn into the words through the illustrations. The non-reading child can predict, anticipate, project, identify, observe and question, all higher-level thinking skills, all within the frame of the picture-book.

The field of picture-books is time-honoured, and the market today is expanding. Parents are realizing the need for pre-reading experience, teachers are recognizing the power of the picture-book for learning, and children are aware that they are not frozen out of the print experience, but incorporated into it. Books for babies are a new category that's doing well. These toddler books are popular with new trends in early education. Often simply designed to be read to young children, they teach the children concepts with visuals that help them be part of reading the book. Publishers are always looking for new concepts, unique ideas, unusual slants to attract children and adults to the book. Many new writers fail to understand that the simplicity of the picture-book requires great skill for success. When one surveys a collection of contemporary successful picture-books, one notices that they represent an enormous range of artistic and literary strengths. Mawkish sentiment, cutesy pictures and trite plots have disappeared; in their place, the child meets a sophisticated story.

The audience for picture-books is complex: we buy them for children, but we buy them for our own interests as well. Teachers, librarians, grand-parents and parents and friends are the main purchasers of picture-books, yet it is the child we must have in mind. Authors must please the child yet not alienate the adult. Because of the limited number of pages and words, everything on every page matters. While the length of lines may be spare, the language and ideas must be rich in sound and in meaning. A picture-book is a combination of a short story, a poem, an essay, and a photo album. Generally, these books are read to children, not by children; but later on, in higher grades, children may read them to younger children, and find the deeper levels of meaning present in all good picture-books.

In creating a picture-book, you as an author must decide on the format: will it be a storybook, an information book, or a concept book that explains how things fit together? Of course, the picture-book can be an interesting hybrid; all three of these categories can be found in many individual books. The type of pictures you use to illustrate your story will largely determine the success of the book. Will you be your own illustrator, or work in tandem with an artist? Will you create a book without words at all? These are the questions you'll have to work through if you are to have a successful book for children. The authors of the selections in this section, who represent the range of picture-books available for children, attempt to explain their philosophies of creating picture-books for young people.

The Emotional Link

Ian Wallace

For the author and illustrator of picture-books, the search to discover "the place where the story belongs" is a protracted experience along a path littered with half-baked notions and false starts, fraught with exultant highs and dangerous lows. Rarely is a book born out of a single resonant idea that emerges fully realized from the start. During the crucial period of the search, the author and/or illustrator must keep a keen eye out for the emotional link to the reader. An elusive creature, it almost never presents itself quickly, but rather appears only after scrupulous delving beneath the story's skin to its heart.

The emotional link is at the core of all book-making. Without it, the reader is left with an accumulation of words and a series of images. In the world of the picture-book, the fundamental task of the author, and on occasion to a greater degree of the illustrator, is to develop an emotional link between the book's characters and the reader, drawing out the reader's response, not in a manipulative way, but through a natural evolution. The author's and illustrator's touch must be so devilishly light—so sure, working in consort with one another—that the reader doesn't notice the strings being pulled.

A larger percentage of authors understand the emotional component in text than do illustrators in illustration. Far too often techniques and visual gimmicks take precedence over thought and careful consideration of the appropriate means and media to evoke a story's sensibilities. Thus the reader has been treated to too many books to which he or she has enormous difficulty relating on any level of understanding. The lack of an emotional link lies at the root of the problem.

Lovers of children's literature are well aware of "the beautiful book"—the book resplendent with illustrations, so overwhelming with its singular beauty that we stand in awe of its technical brilliance. The text quite frequently becomes a minor character in the bid for the limelight. Fortunately, time, with its ability to yellow edges, affords the reader the chance to study, reflect, and analyse. The reader will ultimately realize the "the emperor has no clothes." The flash appeal of form over content will vaporize under closer scrutiny. An emotional link had never been established, and the reader had been cheated out of an enriching experience.

To discover the emotional link of a story, the illustrator must understand all the levels on which the story functions: intellectual, physical, psychological, and spiritual. This link is then made by a variety of means: appropriate media, colour, changing perspectives, shape of the illustrations, shape of the book, style of type, white space around the type and the drawings, and the position of the characters in relationship to one another. Nothing must be left to chance.

In creating the drawings for *Chin Chiang and the Dragon's Dance,* I employed colour as the emotional barometer of the text. This colour-barometer conveys to the reader the emotional link of the story—Chin Chiang's vulnerability and his lack of self-confidence. The colour also lets the reader feel Chin Chiang's conflict change as his confidence grows and the story progresses. This colour device was set within a format whose formal tone was illicited by the text, the design of the book, the dragon motif found in the border of each illustration, and the fine black ink line drawing. The colour unfolds from the opening of the story to its conclusion and evolves over the course of the day, from the soft earth tones during the post-dawn hours, progressing to stronger ones as night falls over the city. As the emotional conflict builds in Chin Chiang, the colour becomes more vivid, reaching its dramatic peak at the climax of the story when Chin Chiang and Pu Yee dance triumphantly through the gates of harmony under a brilliant red sky.

The emotional barometer is supported in its task by the changing perspectives. At two key points, the reader is perched far above the protagonist. The perspective implies Chin Chiang's vulnerability and increases the power of the dragon and the reader. In the spiral staircase drawing, even though Chin Chiang is portrayed to be running away from his family and his responsibilities, he is in fact running straight along the back of the dragon, step by step, scale by scale.

Each of my books has demanded a different style of illustration. The intricate detail of *Chin Chiang and the Dragon's Dance* was inappropriate for *Very Last First Time,* an Inuit tale. The two cultures were totally different in character, history, and landscape. The style of illustration had to change to capture a different people and their story. I knew that the images had to conjure up distinct images that were truly Canadian—hence, the strong influence of our historical painters: Maurice Cullen, J.W. Morrice, Cornelius Krieghoff and the Group of Seven.

This tale presented a classic structure in children's literature— the use of two worlds. I employed two dominant colours to reflect the distinct, yet inseparable worlds entered by Eva Padlyat. The above-ground world is light, thus yellow (also the light from her candle), and the under-ice world is dark, thus purple. (The Inuit refer to the land in which they live as the Land of Purple Twilight.) This colour concept is obvious to the reader upon picking up the book. The world of light (yellow) is captured within the squarish shape of the cover and contrasted sharply with the rectangular, claustrophobic world of dark (purple) of the end papers.

In books like *Chin Chiang and the Dragon's Dance* and *Very Last First Time* research is essential during the creation process. Throughout the period of discovery in Eva's story, the significance of the spirit world to everyday life came clearly into focus. I would have been shirking my responsibility as an illustrator—a storyteller in pictures—if I had overlooked this aspect of Inuit life. My decision to incorporate this fundamental aspect into the under-ice world brought out the fact that the spirits contained there had to be drawn from Eva's perception of what a wolf, bear and seal sea monster would look like, not from mine. Further, they had to be drawn as if by an artist of the eastern Arctic since western Arctic artists draw in a distinctly different style.

The discovery of this world provided me with the emotional link to the story that took the reader far beyond the fear of the dark, the under-ice world, and the ominous, absent sea. The realization and acceptance of this "third world" as an integral part of Inuit life gave Eva's miraculous circular journey a "third story" within the context of the illustrations' language. Readers are haunted and intrigued by the spiritual world as Eva goes about her routine task of gathering up mussels from the ocean floor. Beyond the inherent fear of enclosed spaces and the absent sea, which sits just outside the edges of the book for the majority of the story, the acceptance of the spirit world, found in the ice formations and the shadows, casts a disquieting spell over Eva's adventure, and ultimately over the reader.

An author's and illustrator's foremost responsibility is to the story, not to themselves or each other, not to their editor or publisher, and not even to the reader, although he/she stands next in line. This responsibility demands and deserves the best work each creator can do, conceived after careful thought, born out of scrupulous research, and realized in words and pictures natural to the story. Finding the emotional link is the key, and its discovery will make the search a journey worth taking for both the creator(s) and the reader.

Illustrating the Text

Laszlo Gal

Each year around Christmas the newspapers and magazines start reviewing the newly published Canadian children's books. Usually their articles praise the tremendous growth in the quality and quantity of the Canadian children's book publishing industry, which has really been remarkable, especially if one considers the fact that its rise happened in the last twelve to fifteen years.

It began with a handful of publishing companies who had faith in a few dedicated artists. These artists (who were compelled to find a steady job in order to make ends meet) had to work weekends and late nights on their books, month after month, yet these men and women get much less recognition than they really deserve; the Canada Council Visual Arts Department might not even acknowledge their existence. For instance, the pioneer of Canadian children's book illustrations, Elizabeth Cleaver, deserved Canada's highest honour for her work in this field, but probably she wasn't even known by those who give out the Order of Canada.

It was a very slow and painful process, but it was the beginning of something important and it was a far cry from my early years in Canada in the 1950s when anyone who wanted to do illustrations for children's books had no chance whatsoever.

On December 12th, 1956, the Canadian ocean liner, *Empress of Britain* arrived at St. John from Liverpool with 500 Hungarian refugees on board. I was one of them. A reporter from a local paper came aboard to interview people, and when he found out that I had done a few sketches on the revolution, he bought one for the paper. It was published the same day and I got twenty dollars for the drawing. That was a lot of money in 1956 and I thought I had it made, but almost fifteen years would pass before I would have my first significant children's book published.

The situation was very bleak for artists and illustrators in particular. But in 1958 I got a job as a graphic designer with the CBC, which I held until 1965 when I received an offer from an Italian publishing company to illustrate children's books. I signed a four-year contract and my wife and I moved to Italy.

The books I had to illustrate were ancient heroic sagas retold for children; stories from the ninth and tenth centuries about heroes like Roland, Siegfried and El Cid, and Greek epic poems such as the Iliad, and the Odyssey and the Aeneid.

With seventy illustrations for each book, I had plenty of illustrating to do for the next four years. During this period I learned about colours, how they react and interact with each other; I learned about shapes, style, technique, materials, mediums and so forth by doing and redoing illustrations until I thought I had them right. Then I realized that each story should be approached from a different angle, with a different style.

It is an unwritten rule that an artist should have a distinct style of his or her own, and thus he or she can be recognized instantly by the brush strokes, by the forming of characters, by choice of colour, layout and so on. It is accepted without debate because it's logical and natural, yet this important style that an artist should acquire might also put him or her in a pigeon-hole.

To approach each story from a different direction can be fun and can upgrade the appearance of the book significantly. For instance, one would handle an ancient Greek story differently from the medieval epics of *Beowulf* or the *Nibelungenlied*.

Adapting the style of the period in which the story evolves, the use of design elements, colour, layout and so forth all add flavour and authenticity to the book.

Let's take the *Nibelungenlied* with the stories of Siegfried, Brunhild and Hagen which were written in the middle ages; using a modern illustrative style, technique, or even choice of material can have an adverse effect on the appearance of the book. On the other hand, by creating the characters of the story in the style of the period, the artist can achieve a flavour of authenticity and bring the story and images one step closer to each other.

The artist can get inspiration from the illuminations of medieval manuscripts or from the ancient frescos that decorate the Romanesque churches of northern Italy, Spain and France.

During the last thousand years, from a limited range of colours (raw siennas, umbers, ochre yellows and some blues and reds), time created on these wall paintings an incredibly rich texture as the peeling layers of paint revealed the previously painted surfaces, and blended all colours into a glorious harmony.

Now, by somehow achieving this effect the illustrator can get that desired flavour of colours which will give an ancient look to the painting. How to get this result will depend on how inventive the artist is, how willing he or she is to spend time on experimenting with different media. So when I started to work on the medieval stories for Mondadori, I experimented for weeks with acrylics, tempera, gouache, etc. I even tried every gimmick I could think of such as blotting on the colours, or painting on an overlay and then printing wet colour on the board and thus obtaining a certain texture. However, nothing seemed to work to my satisfaction. Finally, accidentally, I stumbled upon something. As sections of the illustration started to look overcrowded (caused by too much layering of paint), I took a razor blade and began scraping off the thick pigment. Suddenly I realized that I had in front of me a blend of all the colours that I had applied previously and a very similar texture to the Romanesque wall paintings. For the next year and a half, I painted layers upon layers just to scrape them off mercilessly so as to achieve the desired effect.

A few years later I had to start the experiment all over to find a suitable style for the next series of books: the Iliad, the Odyssey, and the Aeneid. The simple vase paintings of the ancient Greeks were what I followed as a style for those stories. The figures on these vases are beautifully stylized and gracefully outlined with sharp, thin white lines. After weeks of experiments I came up with some kind of a solution. Instead of underpainting with gouache as I had done for the medieval illustrations, I applied oil pastel on a white gesso ground and then painted over it with gouache. This combination gave me a soft background into which I scored those very important white outlines.

Each book brings new problems and new challenges. For several reasons *The Willow Maiden* presented a very special challenge. It is a romantic tale set in the middle of a dense forest. The composition, the "staging" and the costumes had to convey the romantic flavour of the tale. What posed the greatest problem was the fact that the story took place on a moonlit midsummer night. This put limitations on the colour range and narrowed it down to blues and greens. For this reason, throughout the book I had to suppress my desire to use colours more freely.

The Enchanted Tapestry brought similar challenges in regard to the colour range, but even more so in composition because I decided to follow the examples of ancient Chinese scrolls. Since the artists did not apply perspective as we know it today on these silk paintings, I tried to design my compositions according to the rules these Chinese masters followed in order to create foreground, middle ground, and background.

When I was a young high-school student, my dream was to

become a stage actor. I attended the Academy of Dramatic Arts but soon realized I didn't quite have the talent for performing. My love for the theatre is still with me and perhaps it is this love that attracts me to tales from historical time periods. I believe an illustrator has to be a costume designer, set designer and an actor all in one, for he or she must put characters in a setting that not only tells a story but is also filled with emotions and feelings.

Images of the North

Ted Harrison

The area North of Sixty comprises a land rich in its variety of land-scapes, peoples and natural life. One cannot generalize about it. The effect it has on a writer and artist is one which generates a great curiosity and desire to fathom the wonderful depths of story and visual delights which are there. Indeed the North can be likened to a festive table laden with such a variety of dishes that the only problem becomes one of choice. Where should one start in this vast array of delights?

When I first entered the region of the North, it was via the Alaska Highway en route to the tiny village of Carcross in the Yukon Territory. As a family we had journeyed from Malaysia to New Zealand and thence to Britain, finally discovering the vastness of Canada and the beauty of the Yukon.

To one whose childhood and adolescent years were spent under the shadow of a coal mine whose single chimney served to darken lungs as well as bricks, the North meant freedom. Freedom to breathe fresh mountain air, to drink water direct from crystal clear lakes, and to gaze upon horizons untainted by the smog of industry.

The North began to weave its magic upon me from the start. My boyhood sense of adventure was rekindled, and a new energy began to take the place of a certain ennui which life further south had engendered. Each object in nature, no matter how small or how large, was beginning to be seen with a new clarity of vision and understanding.

The first thing to be sacrificed was my style of painting, which, until then, had been rather academic and representational in manner. The moment of truth arrived shortly after we had settled into the Carcross teacherage. There all around us were scenes to delight the most jaded eye. Mountain peaks flaunted their snowy crests even at the height of summer, whilst numerous lakes and rivulets glistened under the sun's benign presence. Winter was still an unknown factor as I collected my painting equipment and drove out to the heights surrounding the valley. Here I could see vast stretches of the landscape reaching to the borders of the Alaskan Panhandle.

My tiny sketching stool was firmly planted on the gravel surface, and the easel anchored with a stone to steady it against the breeze blowing in from Lake Bennett. I fixed my eyes on an area to paint, mixed the medium on the palette, and applied the brush with some vigour to the canvas. Everything seemed to be going well until I became aware of a strong subtle force emanating from the land itself. I was being dictated to by this vast panorama. My strength of will was being slowly sapped by these supposedly inanimate objects. Spruce trees, bushes, rocks and mountains were all conspiring to make me paint them in their colours and in their particular forms. Deep inside of me I felt a spark of rebellion being fanned into flame. Soon I knew that my style of painting and my method of seeing were useless in this northern world. My vision had been nurtured in some alien art school far from the Shangri-La I had now chosen as home.

Sadly I packed up the paint tubes and brushes. Loading all the material of creativity into my old station wagon, I drove back to the security of the family. Never again, I resolved, would I tackle Nature head on. I had been defeated and knew it. Yet I desired even more fervently to paint the North and capture some of its spirit on canvas. Like Saul of Tarsus I had been on a mission. Mine was to paint this remarkable land. How to do it remained a mystery until I stopped straining and struggling for an answer and just relaxed. The landscape gradually simplified itself in my perception and I began to see it as a vast ocean upon which people and buildings floated like tiny argosies heading for some distant port. My mind rid itself of all the academic niceties I had been taught; and I began to paint like a "mere" neophyte, not only being introduced for the first time to the arts of painting and drawing, but also to the world.

For the first time in my life I actually began to enjoy the thrill of creating a new vision on canvas. All detail was excluded and the scenes with their tiny figures were portrayed as if some child had taken over the brush. So simple had my style become that I hesitated to paint the mountains and the sky. As time went by the mountains and the sky were tentatively introduced and took their place with the cabins, people, dogs and ravens that made up the world of Carcross.

As the years progressed, I became more and more aware of the remarkable power of colour when applied to simple forms. There arose a new sense of wonderment and freedom. Why not have blue moose, pink dogs, rainbow-like skies? "Saul" had certainly seen the light, and was now revelling in a new world of colour and form that had formerly remained unknown. Each change in my paintings came as a mystery, unforced and hitherto undiscovered. The black lines encompassing my forms gave way to coloured lines of variety and rhythm. The North had indeed worked its magic. Not only had it served to liberate my mind, it had also liberated my mode of seeing. I began to feel as if I'd emerged from some strange chrysalis.

Writing followed in the path of my new creative discovery. One could also "paint" with words about a personal vision of the North. As my first subject I chose the games and recreational sports of the children whom I taught. Snowshoeing was a popular pastime, as were fishing, hunting and trapping. In spring the hardy game-guide horses emerged from the hills and were ridden bareback by the more courageous boys. During "Discovery Days" in Dawson City many children dressed up in costumes reminiscent of the Gold Rush days. Some even panned for gold in Bonanza Creek and were able to find "colour," small nuggets, in their pans. All this material made a rich subject both to write about and illustrate.

The more I observed the environment the more I saw to record. Wonderful stories of the past and present were told to me by many people, and I realized that the North had worked its magic alike on old-timers, the "Sourdoughs," and newcomers, "Cheechakos." So I too, like the early gold seekers, discovered rich veins, not of gold but of human interest. Thus the drawing and painting became interwoven with words to produce a personal "tapestry" of the North.

The seasons also create wonderful images unique to the North. When the temperature drops to below -30°C, snow falls like a white powder and is so cold and dry that it becomes almost like sand. There is a wonderful crunchy sound as one walks, and, on a clear cold morning the sound of wood being chopped carries for great distances. Wintertime can be beautiful yet harsh, and one cannot wander far alone without adequate preparations for survival.

Perhaps the greatest thrill the North has to offer is the sight of a full-blown Aurora Borealis, or Northern Lights. It is then that the whole sky becomes alive with interweaving veils of coloured lights flickering and dancing to some celestial rhythm. One Inuk told me that the dancing lights are the spirits of ancestors who play soccer in the sky using the head of a walrus as a ball. It is understandable that such a magical sight can give rise to the most imaginative folktales.

The native people of the North have lived close to nature for centuries and have learned to treat the land and its animals with respect. Modern ways have now taken the place of many old customs. However, the ways of animals and birds can still instil a feeling of wonder and awe in the sensitive person. Ravens can tease domestic dogs with great intelligence and sense of the comic. One bird will attract the dog's attention by doing a little dance close to the food which the dog is about to devour. Immediately the dog will lunge towards the offending raven, thus giving a second raven the chance to dive in and snatch the morsel. Garbage can lids are sometimes prised off by the huge black birds, causing the contents to be scattered and picked upon at will.

Writers such as Jack London and Robert W. Service have captured the spirit of the North in both poetry and prose. Yet there still remain new stories to tell and new mysteries to puzzle the mind and stimulate the observer. Many images in the North remain constant while others change. It will always be the nature of this land to attract the adventurous and inspire the creative mind.

L'Illustration pour enfants
Stéphane Poulin

Introduction

Dans le livre pour enfants, qu'est-ce qui fait qu'une illustration est bonne ou mauvaise (pour employer des termes simples à sa description)? Qu'est-ce qui fait qu'elle répond au courant actuel, qu'elle est dépassée ou qu'elle semble à l'abri de toute mode, compte tenu du fait que l'enfant évolue à travers les âges et que ses besoins et préoccupations changent.

Quelle est la recette pour créer une illustration que l'on aimera à coup sûr?

Il n'existe point, à mon humble avis, de critères pour évaluer objectivement l'illustration. Puisqu'il n'y a pas d'écoles pour l'enseigner, l'illustration pour enfants échappe à toute étiquette, tout courant de pensée. C'est ce qui explique, probablement, sa grande variété de styles. C'est ce qui fait sa force aussi puisqu'elle est en mutation constante et se moque bien des recettes miracles.

L'illustration est, d'après moi, une interprétation personnelle de la réalité et de l'imaginaire de l'artiste.

Ma critique et mon approche face à l'illustration se basent sur une expérience personnelle d'abord et avant tout. L'illustration est pour moi un véhicule de la pensée, un art communicatif qui s'adresse à un public bien précis. Dans ce cas-ci, il s'agit des enfants.

Que raconte l'illustration dans le livre pour enfants?

Mon choix (puisque c'est un choix) au départ était de dessiner pour le simple plaisir de la chose. Dès mes premières expériences, illustrer pour les enfants s'est avéré correspondre à mon désir le plus cher; qui était de partager ce qu'il y avait de plus important à mes yeux. Communiquer et témoigner de la vie et des gens qui m'entouraient.

Le livre pour enfants est pour moi un moyen idéal de renvoyer aux gens une image constructive d'eux-mêmes, sans être toutefois trop sentimental et idéaliste envers la condition humaine. Je crois que l'homme et la femme ont souvent une vision négative d'eux-mêmes et de leur environnement, ce qui a pour effet qu'ils cherchent à s'en éloigner, et du fait même ils s'en déracinent et en oublient le sens profond.

Ceci m'amène à parler du discours que véhicule généralement le livre pour enfants tant sur le plan du texte que de l'illustration. À ce niveau,

Illustrating for Children
Stéphane Poulin

Introduction

What makes an illustration in a children's book good or bad (to use simple descriptive terms)? What makes it current, out-of-date or seemingly ageless, given the fact children evolve over the generations and their needs and concerns change?

What is the recipe for creating an illustration that everyone will like?

In my humble opinion, there are no criteria for objectively evaluating an illustration. Since there are no schools that teach it, children's illustration falls outside of artistic labels and trends. And this is probably the reason for the tremendous variety of existing styles. This is also its strength, since children's illustration is constantly evolving and needs no secret recipe.

Illustration, as I see it, is a personal interpretation of the artist's reality and imagination.

My own approach to it is based on personal experience. For me, illustration is a vehicle for my thoughts, a communicative art that addresses itself to a very specific audience; in this case, to children.

What Do Illustrations Communicate in a Children's Book?

At the beginning, my choice (since it is a choice) was to draw for the sheer pleasure of it. From my very first experiences, illustrating for children proved to satisfy my most cherished desire, that is, to share what I felt to be important. To communicate and give expression to the life and the people around me.

For me, children's books are an ideal method of transmitting back to people a constructive image of what they are, without, however, being too sentimental and idealistic about the human condition. I think that men and women often have a negative vision of themselves and of their environment. The effect of this is that they try to distance themselves from their surroundings and become uprooted, thus forgetting the meaning of life.

This leads me to discuss the message that children's books generally convey, both in terms of text and illustration. On this level, I would classify books into two major categories, that is as relating two distinct

je me permettrais de classifier le livre en deux grandes catégories, soit deux discours bien distincts quoique non dissociables nécéssairement.

Il existe donc deux types de livres que j'appelerais: «Le livre fantastique ou poétique» et «Le livre d'histoires vraies ou vraisemblables».

Dans le premier cas, l'histoire et les personnages correspondent à un monde fictif, créé de toute pièce par l'auteur. Rien n'y est réel et ne peut se rapporter au vécu quotidien de l'enfant, sauf peut-être le message, qui par ses clins d'œil, invite l'enfant à y pénétrer. Cette forme de langage est très délicate puisque dans certains cas, les fantasmes et la vision de l'artiste ne tiennent absolument pas compte du vécu actuel de l'enfant. Il en résulte une gratuité dans le message puisque celui-ci est à sens unique. L'histoire «vole» trop haut et n'atterrit jamais pour permettre aux voyageurs d'y monter.

Cependant, dans le cas où l'auteur tend la main au lecteur, une complicité magique s'établit. L'enfant s'installe dans le récit et s'identifie volontiers à l'histoire. Il en résulte une stimulation de la propre créativité de l'imaginaire chez l'enfant. À partir de modèles, il crée ses propres scénarios. Par exemple, il inventera de nouveaux mots pour désigner des choses du commun.

Le second type de livre, dit «Histoires vraisemblables», fait plutôt référence au vécu quotidien et réel de l'enfant. Ce type de récit met en scène de véritables personnages à l'intérieur d'un cadre de vie tout aussi réel. Le message y est principalement axé sur les préoccupations de l'enfant et met en relief les expériences d'un quotidien accessibles à tous. Une fois de plus ce type de discours comporte des pièges.

En effet, dans certains cas l'histoire renvoie le lecteur à des modèles établis et à un quotidien morne et ennuyeux. C'est le type d'histoire qui endort assurément les enfants le soir venu. Le message se complaît dans les grandes vérités ne laissant point de place à l'interprétation.

Il existe finalement une tierce possibilité qui tend à un mariage des deux discours, soit une évocation des expériences réelles d'un personnage réel dans un cadre tout à fait fictif, soit l'apparition d'un personnage fictif (peut-être un animal personnifié) dans un cadre bien réel. Cela permet au lecteur de transcender les modèles dans un monde qui est bien le sien. L'environnement offre désormais d'infinies possibilités de lieux imaginaires.

Quant à moi, je préfère davantage cette dernière approche puisqu'elle valorise l'éveil du lecteur à son environnement. Elle lui ouvre une fenêtre sur le monde extérieur.

Comme je le mentionnais au tout début, il n'existe quand même aucun critère objectif pour juger un livre. L'approche humaine de l'au-

messages, which are not mutually exclusive.

Hence, there are two types of books, which I would call "fantastic or poetic books" and "real or realistic storybooks."

In the first case, the story and the characters are fictitious, created all of a piece by the author. Nothing is real in this story and it does not relate to the daily life of the child, except perhaps through its message, which it subtly invites the child to penetrate. Using the language in this way is a very delicate process, since in some cases the artist's imagination and vision do not take into account the child's daily life. There is a certain gratuitousness about the message since it works in only one direction. The story "flies" too high and never lands to allow the travellers to embark.

However, when the author holds out a hand to the reader, a magic complicity is established. The child enters the story and willingly identifies with it. The result is a stimulation of the child's own creativity and imagination. Based on the models in the story, the child creates his or her own scenarios, inventing, for example, new words to describe ordinary objects.

The second type of book, called the realistic story, refers rather to the child's real and actual daily experiences. This type of story presents real characters within the framework of an equally real life. The message is based mainly on the child's concerns and relies on the daily experiences that are accessible to all. But this type of story has its own traps.

Indeed in certain cases the story refers the reader to established models and to an everyday life that is dull and boring. This is the type of story that is sure to put children to sleep at night. The message delights in morals which leave no room for interpretation.

Finally, there is a third possibility: a mixture of the previous two, arrived at by conjuring up the real experiences of a real character in a completely fictional setting, or by the apparition of a fictional character (perhaps an animal personified) in a very real setting. This allows the reader to transcend the models in his or her own world. Henceforth, the child's surroundings offer infinite possibilities for imaginary places.

Personally, I prefer this last approach since it emphasizes bringing the reader into greater contact with his or her surroundings. It opens a window to the outside world.

As I mentioned at the beginning, there is no objective criteria for judging a book. The author's human approach determines in large part the illustration's credibility. Unless you attempt a theoretical criticism

teur détermine en grande partie de la crédibilité de l'illustration.

A moins de tenter une critique théorique de l'image, fondée sur les théories de la composition et des couleurs et leurs rapports . . . À moins de s'en tenir à une lecture linéaire de l'image et de sa classification aux mouvements picturaux existants . . . À moins de n'être plus tout à fait un enfant qui ne juge pas, mais aime ou n'aime pas . . . Là, vous trouverez matière à critiquer.

L'image et sa conception

Le rôle de l'illustrateur est de transposer sur papier des images qui proviennent de l'imaginaire. C'est là toute la difficulté. Bien des gens croient qu'une image s'ébauche lors de son exécution sur papier et qu'il suffit d'avoir des notions en dessin pour les réaliser. C'est tout à fait faux. Avant même de bâtir l'esquisse, l'illustrateur doit déjà posséder une image mentale du sujet, du moins, en ce qui me concerne . . .

Pour moi, une image reste irréalisable tant que je n'en possède pas tous les détails en mémoire. Au bout d'un moment, l'image m'apparaît enfin et se fixe en moi. Tant et aussi longtemps qu'elle restera dans ma tête, aucun détail ne peut plus s'effacer. Cette représentation mentale tend même à se préciser davantage avec le temps. Voilà qu'entrent en jeu les techniques d'illustration; c'est-à-dire que je dois maintenant tenter de reproduire physiquement les impressions et l'atmosphère de cette image mentale.

En ce qui me concerne, le résultat final d'une illustration me satisfait pleinement que lorsqu'elle est la transposition fidèle de mon idée originale. Pour vous en expliquer le sens, c'est un peu comme lorsque vous faites une recette de sauce à spaghetti . . . vous mélangez une foule d'ingrédients dans une grosse marmitte en dosant minutieusement chacun d'eux afin d'obtenir la saveur recherchée.

Quant aux lois et principes du dessin, on se rend compte qu'ils ne sont pas nécessairement applicables, ou du moins logiques, quand on tente de reproduire une image mentale bien précise. L'imaginaire ne tenant pas compte de certaines théories, il faut donc tricher constamment et amputer ici et là.

L'illustration est composée de «tricheries» dont il faut apprendre les ficelles.

Cette dernière étape de la conception dépend entièrement de la perception et de la créativité de l'illustrateur.

Une fois l'image mentale transposée, il ne reste plus qu'à élaborer une mise en scène où les personnages et les lieux apparaissent comme ayant été photographiés sur le vif. C'est-à-dire que l'illustration doit

of the drawing, based on theories of the composition of colours and their inter-relationship . . . . Or unless you stick to a linear reading of the drawing and classify it within existing pictorial movements . . . . Or unless you are no longer completely a child who doesn't judge but who likes or dislikes . . . . In these cases you will find material for criticism.

The Image and Its Conception

The role of the illustrator is to transpose onto paper images which come from the imagination. This is where the difficulty arises. Many people believe that an image acquires shape as it is put down on paper and that all that is needed are basic drawing techniques. This is completely false. As far as I am concerned, even before constructing a rough sketch, the illustrator must already have an image in mind, at least of the main subject.

For me, a drawing remains unrealizable as long as I don't have all the details in my mind. After a while, the image finally comes to me and engages my attention. For as long as it remains in my mind, no detail can be erased. This mental image tends to become more precise over time. At this point the techniques of illustration come into play. That is to say that I now have to try to reproduce the impressions and the surroundings of this mental image on paper.

In my case, the final result of an illustration satisfies me completely only when it is a faithful transposition of my original idea. Let me explain what I mean. It's rather like when you prepare a spaghetti sauce: you combine many different ingredients in a large pot, carefully measuring each one of them in order to produce the desired flavour in the end.

As to the laws and principles of drawing, it becomes obvious that they are not necessarily applicable or even logical as soon as you try to reproduce a very specific mental image. Imagination does not tend to take theories into account . . . . So you have to cheat constantly and take liberties here and there.

Illustration is made up of tricks and you have to know the ropes.

This last stage of conception depends completely on the illustrator's perception and creativity.

So, once the mental image is transposed, all that is left to develop is a setting in which the characters and places appear as though they had been photographed from life. That is, an illustration should represent a sequence and not a still shot, otherwise the image seems to be waiting for us to look at it. It becomes static and lifeless.

présenter une séquence et non un arrêt de l'action, sinon l'image semble attendre qu'on la regarde. Elle devient statique et sans vie.

Une image doit nous donner l'impression du mouvement suspendu dans le temps. Elle doit nous laisser croire que les personnages voyagent d'une page à l'autre du livre.

L'enfant tourne alors les pages afin de *suivre* le récit et non à fin de l'animer.

Le livre pour enfants renferme de grandes richesses, si ce n'est que de nous raconter. Le livre en lui-même n'est rien, c'est aux lecteurs de lui donner un rôle. Le livre se lit, il se raconte, il se mime, il est tout ce qu'on veut en faire. À vous d'en épuiser les ressources.

A drawing should give us the impression of movement suspended in time. It should let us believe that the characters are travelling from one page to another in the book.

Then the child turns the pages in order to follow the story and not in order to give life to it.

A children's book contains incredible riches, if only in what it tells us about ourselves. The book itself is nothing, the reader must give it a role. The book is read, told, acted out; it can be anything you want. It's up to you to exhaust its resources.

2

Writing for the Beginning Reader

Introduction

Today's children are anxious for meaning in what they read. They are not content with decoding simplistic words to arrive at unimportant information. If they have had a diet of exciting picture-books from caring adults, they will want to make the reading leap with the same powerful language and ideas that they have heard and seen.

Often these books are labelled "easy-read," "fun-to-read," "beginning-readers" or "read-along," so that the child understands that he or she will be involved in the reading of the words as well as in interpreting the visuals. This is a growth market in writing for children today. However, publishers generally don't accept books where the word count or the word control overrides the quality of the literature. It is an extremely delicate balance to draw the child into the book without presenting too many obstacles. However, there are many types of books that beginning readers can enjoy: books of memorable selections, poems and songs that children already have in their memory banks; stories they have heard before, so they can bring background knowledge into the reading process; stories with recurring chunks of language so that once the first section has been understood, the next sequence falls into place; stories with strong picture meanings, so the child can continue to use the picture clues to assist in the reading; a rebus, a story in which a picture is inserted in place of the word; stories with strong endings that encourage the child to continue reading—riddles, jokes, and mysteries that are finally explained.

The authors in this section explore patterned picture-books for young children, early readers, and beginning novels. The essays demonstrate the wide range of books that are now available for the beginning reader.

Writing Easy-Reads for Juvenile Readers

Susan Wallace

In a children's bookstore recently I watched while a customer picked up a copy of Judy Blume's *The One in the Middle is a Green Kangaroo.* She read it to the end in four minutes flat. Then she turned to her companion and said, "That's a cute story. Very simple really. I bet authors make a lot of money churning these things out. I could probably whip up one or two of them a week. Anybody could write this stuff."

Would that this were true!

> The author of a good easy-read book
> makes the book so readable
> that writing for kids
> looks like kids' stuff.

But easy-read books are most definitely not easy-write books. They are written for children who have just begun to read silently on their own. Children who, up to the moment they pick up their first easy-read, have relied a great deal on illustrations to assist them in unlocking new vocabulary and in understanding the story. They are motivated to move on from picture-books to novels because that's what they see older children and adults reading. They like the idea of holding in their hands a book that looks like a grown-up novel. But when they start such a book, these seven-, eight- and nine-year-olds do so with shaky confidence that they will be able to read it. The adult-novel size and intriguing full-colour cover will grab them but it will not hold them for long.

Your job as a writer is to get them quickly hooked on the story and to make the story so readable, so smooth, clear and engaging, that their confidence as readers is never shaken from page one to the end. The story must also deliver an emotional experience satisfying enough to children that for the time of the read it can compete with all surrounding temptations: friends, computers, videos and even the children's old comfort level with picture-books. If it does not, your book will quickly be abandoned for these other pursuits and you will have failed as an author.

You must accomplish all this in about two thousand to thirty-five hundred words. You can count on only a few simple illustrations to augment the meaning delivered by the printed word. You must accomplish all this and still produce a story that can stand on its own as a fine piece of literature.

Nothing to it, right? Kids' stuff!

Before I go any further, a word of reassurance to those of you out there who—despite the demands I've just outlined—still think you'd like to try this kind of writing. The sensitivities and techniques needed to produce the consummate level of readability required in an easy-read book can be studied and learned. Techniques are, of course, no substitute for talent. What you have to say matters as much as how you say it. No one can give you the imagination and wit to think up irresistible stories that spark the interest of young readers. But assuming you have the storyteller's talent, this chapter may help you write with the smoothness and clarity needed by young readers.

In the world of adult reading, if you have something wonderful to say, the committed reader will bear with a lot of unreadable material before giving up on you as an author. No one would try to claim Franz Kafka wrote highly readable material. But the commitment beginning readers have to reading is tenuous and to hold them past page one we have to make the task as easy as possible.

If you asked many successful authors what techniques they use to make their stories for young children highly readable, they would say they weren't aware of any. Some writers have a natural gift for writing readable stories without thinking about how they are doing it. But if you are not one of them and need to learn, as I have had to learn, the art of readability, keep reading.

As a children's author I am a neophyte. It is true I am published and have just won a minor writer's award. But I am still at the point where, when someone refers to me as an author, I feel guilty accepting the title. A title that I think belongs to a Judy Blume or a Gordon Korman but not to me, not just yet. All of which is another way of saying that I probably had no business agreeing to write this article. My publisher assumed that since I had gone through the process of getting started as an author of easy-read books for children I could readily tell others how to do it. I was too vain to call him back and give him reason to assume otherwise. So here I was getting ready to tell people how to do something I wasn't sure I knew how to do myself . . . .

Getting started produced some interesting results. I had to think back over my brief writing career to take a hard look at what I have been doing that has gotten me into print. I discovered I am applying in my writing knowledge and techniques gained from years of teaching experience and the reading of hundreds of children's stories. The knowledge and techniques I'm referring to here have nothing to do with writing mechanics. You can learn those elements of writing far better from more accomplished authors. The knowledge I have to share relates to the sensitivity you need to develop towards your young readers. This sensitivity along with a few simple techniques will help you choose what to write about and ensure that you don't build your stories on concepts or use vocabulary not readily understood by young readers. It will also help you develop believable characters with which children can readily identify. Above all, it will enable you to tailor your material to the unique but often dimly understood demands of the early reading experience.

Task one, acquiring sensitivity, requires getting to know your readers. It means spending time with them and the books they prize.

The first stories I wrote were less than professional. Parts of them seemed engaging and readable. Other parts didn't seem to work. I began to read and reread all the easy-read books I knew kids loved. Then I watched children read these books on their own and chatted with them about their personal reactions to the stories. I began to give the children my own materials to read. There is no more humbling experience than to see a child put down—after one minute—the creation you have sweated over and concluded was quite good. Watch while that same child immediately picks up some other author's book and stays with it to the end with that *must read* look on his face. A painful experience? Yes. But I know of no faster way to acquire the reader sensitivity some writers seem to have intuitively. These writers seem to know as they write how their readers are going to respond. But sensitivity can be acquired by careful observation of children's responses. For instance, Robert Munsch goes about the country telling his stories to groups of children. He changes them as he learns from the children's responses what works. One of his stories will be told and altered many times before it gets into print. From A.A. Milne to Dennis Lee, you will find a surprising number of children's authors got their start telling stories to children.

From observing children reading your materials, you will quickly ascertain the degree of success you are achieving in making your stories readable. You may find you need to take a more active part in controlling this process. Time to tackle task two in becoming a more reader-sensitive writer, understanding the reading process. You need to know what the child has to do to get meaning from the printed page.

To make sense of what you write the reader must be able to

convert your words into ideas and images. At the same time the reader must also connect each newly processed idea or image to an idea or image already on file in the brain. What's on file in seven-, eight- and nine-year-old brains? Less than adults assume.

Mention that your protagonist is alone on an island, and follow this by the information that the only boat available is drifting away in the storm. The older reader will automatically connect the word "island" to the need for a boat. Already your readers are considering problems that might arise out of this situation. They have grasped the logical relationship between the newly processed idea "boat drifting away" and the image of the island they already have on file.

But what will happen if it turns out your reader hasn't the foggiest notion of what an island is? The connection will not be made. The reader is unable to form the second image. Your reader's brain will have to put this unconnected piece of information on hold. But the brain's holding capacity is more limited than you might think. The more pieces of unconnected material the brain has to carry at any given time, the longer it takes for the brain to connect new ideas and images. Throw into your story two or three concepts your readers don't under-stand and you will lose them completely.

You may think I am belabouring the point here. Any reasonable person would not write about things kids know nothing about. Let me assure you it is oh so easy to assume that kids have knowledge they don't have. The brains of seven-, eight- and nine-year-olds are becom-ing increasingly adept at grasping logical relationships as long as the relationships are based on ideas they already have stored in their brains. These ideas are formed through concrete experience of real things and events. Sometimes pictures can substitute for these expe-riences or enhance a partially formed idea or concept. But easy-read writers have the luxury of only a few, if any, coloured illustrations to clarify concepts crucial to the understanding of their stories. You must ensure that your readers have the knowledge needed to understand your story neatly tucked away in their intellectual storehouses.

Gaining a knowledge of the concepts children have developed by ages seven, eight and nine will have a profound effect on what you choose to write about. Generally, you will be better off if you stick to things that are very close in time and space to the child's everyday world. At first this may seem limiting. But as you explore the interests of this age group—their home, their school, their pets, their friends and the significant adults in their lives—you will begin to feel the great need children have to explore these relationships. They want to be exposed to other children grappling with the same kinds of problems they meet in their own lives. Children are fascinated with story characters who find successful and sometimes amusing or novel solutions to these problems. You will not be writing the Great Canadian Novel. But you will be helping to foster in children feelings of self-worth and high ideals. And you will be assisting them to claim print kinship with humanity.

When you write about things and events your young readers are familiar with, you will find you naturally tend to use vocabulary easily understood by your readers. Note that I did not say vocabulary that is easily read by young readers! In the end they are one and the same. But I choose to make this distinction to remove any possibility you might translate or equate the term "easily read" with easy-to-sound-out or already in the child's sight vocabulary. Control of language to that which is eminently readable by children should not consist of a planned attempt to constrict the language you use to tell your story.

Never attempt to write a children's story using a prescribed set of words that early readers are supposed to be able to recognize with ease. There have been books on the market for years called easy-reads that do just that. You can imagine what literary horrors these monosyllabic books are. I have never seen a child read such a book without teacher prodding.

Just tell your story, taking into account what is likely to be going on in the mind of the young reader, and use language that creates an esthetic experience. Do this and you will find you have not gone far wrong in your choice of readable words and phrases. The sensitivity you are developing towards your readers will soon have you choosing language that logically and comfortably connects a child with his or her past experiences. Write about experiences close to the child and observe the principles of good writing. Control of the language will happen naturally.

Given that you will be mainly writing stories about children's lives, the use of dialogue cannot be avoided. There is no place in your writing where you will find your reader-sensitivity more crucial. To write convincing dialogue you must know how children talk. You need to observe the patterns and rhythms of their speech and to recognize, for instance, that like adults, children talk in fragments and not in complete sentences. Recognize also that they talk to adults differently from the way they talk to their peers.

I am constantly reminded of this difference whenever I hear a child let loose on the playground with a string of swear-words that would do an old navy man proud. When talking to adults, this same child never swears and will only blushingly admit to having ever used a four-letter word. I mention this not because I expect you to have your young characters swearing a blue streak, but to illustrate the difference between peer-group language and the language a child uses with adults. You must be able to put yourself in the shoes of each of the young characters you create and make them talk the way children do. If you don't, your characters will not be believable.

In addition you will have created a major roadblock to reading. The children's flow of reading will be interrupted each time they meet a word in your dialogue they do not recognize by sight. You will have robbed them of their natural way of unlocking new vocabulary.

The good reader is a person who looks at a page of print and begins triggering patterns stored in his or her linguistic memories. Children have down pat all the patterns of how children are supposed to talk. When dialogue is real, children are propelled into anticipating the next word, line or phrase. This releases them to a continuous flow of reading without the traditional vocabulary breakdowns engendered by word-by-word reading.

Using these structures the child is able to figure out much of the new vocabulary he or she encounters. If these natural oral patterns are not respected in your dialogue, if you break the rules of rhythm by not having your children talk *properly,* you will have robbed the language of its natural melodies. This will automatically engender word-by-word reading.

If this happens too often in your writing, the children will be forced to rely on sounding-out as the only method they have at their disposal for figuring out new words. They will quickly decide your book is too hard for them and that reading any further is not worth the effort.

Gaining a knowledge of the reading process will help you to appreciate a relatively new technique that is being used to create readability —chunking. This technique is both powerful and simple to execute.

Reading experts have known for a long time that it isn't the length or number of words in a sentence that determines how easy or difficult a time readers have absorbing the information in that sentence. Rather, it's the number of thoughts your reader's mind has to process within the time it takes to read the sentence. And more than simply the number of the thoughts, the nature and difficulty of the thoughts to be processed.

Experienced readers do not move through a sentence by reading each word separately. They group together the words that best create meaning. To assist young readers to see and sense the groups of words in a sentence that best create meaning and to allow you, the writer, the luxury of presenting more than one thought in a sentence and still be sure that your readers will not have a difficult time reading it, I strongly suggest you adopt the practice of having your stories printed in chunks of meaning. This makes unreadable sentences, such as the one you have just attempted to read, readable. Try reading the same sentence again printed in chunks of meaning.

> To assist young readers
> to see and sense
> the groups of words in a sentence
> that best create meaning
> and to allow you the writer
> the luxury
> of presenting more than one thought in a sentence
> and still be sure that your readers will not have
> > a difficult time reading it
> I strongly suggest
> that you adopt the practice
> of having your stories printed
> in chunks of meaning.

Now I am not suggesting you write convoluted sentences like this one. I am trying to illustrate the use of chunking as a marvellously effective device for creating highly readable material.

The old adage "the more you learn the more you find out you don't know" is very applicable to what may happen to you as your reader-sensitivity grows. You may even find that trying to maintain an awareness of your reader inhibits your writing for a while. Do not get discouraged. It may seem difficult at first but you can train yourself to read what you have written from a child's point of view. Eventually you will find yourself thinking this way automatically and responding as a child would respond, not after you have written, but in the very process of it. Someone may then comment that your writing reads like kids' stuff.

Patterns and Structures for Writing

Maryann Kovalski

There are people, I suspect, who long to write stories for children and sit, like Rodin's *Thinker*, trying to conjure up something that will wow the multitudes. Or else there are those who employ the market research approach: "I want to write something that's never been done before. Hmmm . . . " It's forgivable. Anyone who's longed to make marks on paper with words or pictures has fallen prey to those traps—it's so easy to do. But the results of either approach are almost always stilted and self-conscious. The writer has committed the cardinal sin of anticipating a reaction. Not unlike the five-year-old trying to be cute—it's only embarrassing.

If a story is to be good, it must be, on some level, true. It needn't be a factual retelling of an actual event, though that has proven a successful catalyst for many a good story. It must be from the heart. It must have a universal emotional truth. Later the writer will detach emotionally from the story, and with the help of a good and ruthless editor, the story will become refined and polished.

Finding one's own story, especially in the beginning, often comes out of the writer's own life experiences and interests. I wrote countless bad stories when I was starting out, about little creatures who lived in the forest by the old mill. Essentially retelling tales I loved as a kid. But they were bad stories because they were nothing more than a rehash of another writer's story. I am a city person. For me, the urban sprawl I find myself living in is endlessly fascinating and funny. Finally, I have learned to stick to the landscape I know and love best.

There are always several stories in my head at any given time. Keeping a pocket-size notebook with me always, I record ideas and events. I jot down bits and pieces that I see and hear in restaurants or on the streets. Predicaments people find themselves in in the urban jungle are wonderful fodder. Sometimes two or three little ideas can be incorporated into one good story.

I cannot shout loudly enough how important it is to keep one's eyes open. If you long to write or draw well—you must be willing to look, look and look again with great concentration. If something has been drawn or written well, it is because it has been observed well. It took me years to realize that. In the past I would spend countless hours hunched over my drawing board, drawing and redrawing something inadequately observed in the first place. It was painfully exasperating as it produced only ho-hum work for all my labour. How I wish I had used that time more effectively by getting up and walking and staring at things! Puritan ethic, I suppose. I didn't realize then how well the brain records and stores information, and how nicely it can come spewing out later at the drawing board or typewriter.

Another vital exercise in looking is to look at what others are doing and have done in the field. Make it your business to know this business. Look at every good book from every part of the globe. It's surprising how much one's standards are raised by constant observation of the world's best. I'm always surprised by the gamut of subjects covered in children's literature. An afternoon at a good children's bookstore will have me moved to tears one minute and laughing out loud the next—and quite breathless at the range of ideas covered. Every facet of the human experience is explored. Fear, love, the loss of love, human frailty, vanity, even death—it's all there in sheep's or frog's clothing.

A writer brings a wonderful richness to a work when he or she knows and loves his subject. A mere passing fancy will expose the author's superficiality. Maurice Sendak's love and ever-growing knowledge of the theatre is recorded nicely in his work. Eric Beddows' appreciation of architecture is obvious. William Steig's prescience of human beings and their foibles is made apparent in every story.

Making good stories for children has nothing to do with children —their appreciation is merely a by-product of the work. One of the world's most prominent and well-loved children's book author/illustrators confided in me that he has no fondness for children. Shocking? Not really. In fact, writing stories out of a fondness for children can produce horribly sentimental treacle. It is entirely possible for someone who has no knowledge of or fondness for children to write stories children would adore.

When I was a child, my father's bachelor brother lived with us from time to time, depending on his fortunes. My Uncle Benny was a compulsive gambler who kept us children transfixed with his wonderfully inappropriate stories of his adventures at the track. The man loved the ponies, not children, but oh, how we children loved his stories!

Someone once said, "Rules are meant to be broken, but they are best broken by those who know the rules." It's helpful to stay within an accepted framework as you, the beginning writer, gather your strength as an author. The standard formula of introducing character, followed by conflict, and ending with resolution of conflict still allows a great deal of latitude and can help organize what would otherwise be a hodgepodge of ideas, however witty or clever.

The device the writer uses to introduce the character is where the writer's originality can shine. A character's amusing peccadilloes or telling Achilles' heel can lead nicely into conflict and in fact explain the character's present predicament.

The notion of conflict is also terribly broad. It could be internal (the character's fear of something), or external (the character is attacked or threatened in some way). A change of circumstances or place might signal a conflict. It can be anything, in fact, that challenges the character's mettle.

While the sets of challenges that the writer faces in character development and conflict are indeed awesome, I find resolution the "high jump" of the exercise. I sweat bullets over my endings (though I hope this doesn't show!). When I manage to tie it all up neatly and yet unexpectedly, I feel nothing short of exhilarated.

Because I came to the field as an illustrator first, I've been lucky to have had opportunities that the non-illustrating writer misses. I've been allowed a great deal of on-the-job training as an author while I have illustrated others' work. I've also been fortunate that I've been permitted by my partner, authors and my publisher to go beyond decorating text, that through my pictures I've even changed stories. When I was first given the manuscript to *The Cake That Mack Ate,* I was given it absolutely cold. No meeting with the author, no comment from the publisher. Valerie Hussey and Ricky Englander wanted to see what I could bring to the party. I saw the farmer and his wife as an older couple—that was easy. But I just couldn't see Mack—how he fit into their lives. A nephew? A grandchild? No, it lacked "bite." After a bit, it just seemed to make sense that Mack be their dog. How lucky I was that Rose Robart was delighted!

Because I was an illustrator first, I rely on pictures to tell my stories. I love lots of text but I am sticking to simple sentences while I learn my craft. Perhaps I will always write with pictures, I don't know. I've always thumbnailed (sketched little pictures) as I jot down story ideas. But it has proven a habit that's got me into trouble more than once. I develop a fondness for an image or scene that I desperately want to see happen—sometimes at the peril of the story! When I can't let it go, I've written around it to make the story fit my picture. The tail is wagging the dog, and that's no good.

Of course I'm fooling no one, and with great diplomatic skill my publisher gets me to abandon these nice pictures which do nothing for the story. They are now trying to blindfold me in the early stages and make me resolve the story first. But like the person who needs to talk with his hands, I wonder if I will ever be able to speak without mine—sketching as I think.

Each book affords me a chance for another exploration, another chance to strengthen my skill and to overcome past weaknesses. Each book brings me to a new place. While I still bring my life to my books, all this observing has brought an unexpected richness to my life. My only passion was to become good at what I did—I didn't know it would make me love life more.

Strange, the places those dogs and ducks can take you.

Inviting the Reader Into the Story

Ted Staunton

The hardest invitation to give and the best to receive is one from a writer to a reader. What makes it unique is very simple: it's the only invitation anyone can turn down without an excuse. That means you, the writer, have to make sure that not only is the invitation appealing but that everything you promise gets delivered. Otherwise, readers will just go on up the block to something you weren't invited to and you'll never even know they're gone until you get your royalty cheque.

What can you do to make readers feel welcome enough to stick around? Even if you intend to scare the pants off them? Below are some practical suggestions on four aspects of the problem: what entertains, taste and gender, length, and what "hooks" a reader. With these come some brief theoretic answers, because I feel that what's practical must be clearly based on one's own principles, particularly in a business as laden with compromise as publishing. Without them your invitation will probably get lost in the shuffle.

What Entertains a Child?

Theoretic answer: the same thing that entertains you—a good story, compellingly told. It seems to me that if something you write "for kids" isn't something you'd be interested in reading yourself, you're being pretty condescending to your readers. You might enjoy it for partly different reasons, but then what two readers won't?

Practical answer: stories about their concerns. The problems of children, like those of anyone else, are not trivial. No matter how funny or fantastical, your story must be anchored in a situation that in some way rings true to your reader.

Characters they can identify with. That is, anybody or anything with whom they can share an aspiration or triumph over an insecurity.

A happy ending. The characters your reader identifies with should win out at least partly through their own resources.

Circular or twist endings. In these, the story seems to resolve itself but then a last-page twist will hint that the magic *was* real, or that the same chain of funny events is likely to begin all over again.

The repetition of key words or phrases that are fun to say. These get the very young actively involved as they anticipate, then chant along. Readers like them also, but watch out: overuse reduces enjoyment.

Descriptions based on taste, smell, sound, and touch. Most of us instinctively describe in visual terms first, but appeals to the other senses make writing more vivid. You'll need visual description in a novel, but why bother in a picture-book?

Rhythmic Language. Most books for kids get read aloud, so write for the ear, not the eye. The sounds of your story help build mood and interest. Varying the length and internal order of sentences, careful punctuation, dialogue, and the judicious use of onomatopoeia and alliteration all help with this.

Economy of language. As if the above isn't enough, try to write so that if someone is reading your story to an audience there will be nothing they're tempted to skip.

Is There a Boy–Girl Difference in Creating a Book for an Audience?

Theoretic answer: no. Your job is to make your story interesting to as many different readers as possible.

Practical answer: it depends on what you want to write.

For the youngest, picture-book audience, there is no difference. Publishers define this market by age more than sex.

If you're writing fiction for readers say, eight and up, things change. Girls and boys frequently have different interests and rates of development, but I think their concerns are the same. The stories with the widest appeal recognize this and deal with people, their problems, and how they get along.

Nonetheless, some topics will appeal more to one sex than the other. My publisher says this is fine *as long as there's no unthinking sexism*; they'd aim the book at one segment of the market. This can be an asset, she notes: a book for girls twelve to fourteen might do better than one for boys because most readers that age are girls.

There are also publishers of genre fiction like teen romances, girl or boy detective stories, etc. They, apparently, can tell you exactly what makes a "boy's" or "girl's" book, should you wish to write for them. If your heart or high explosives lie there, go to it.

How Long Should a Book Be?

Theoretic answer: no longer than it needs to be.

Practical answer: picture-books, 0-800 words, novels 20-40 000 words.

To keep down cost, most picture-books are thirty-two pages, cover to cover, or one signature*. Subtracting space for the title page, publishing data, and pictures leaves about fourteen pages for text. Each of these will have one to three brief paragraphs to a total of about twenty, or 800 words.

I split my story into fourteen page "breaks" before submission, and write with more detail than the final text will have. These help indicate what pictures would show, and guide the artist. Later the text is trimmed to complement the pictures.

There are exceptions to all this, but they're expensive. If you're starting out, don't expect one to be made.

As the figures indicate, novel length is more flexible. Novels are cheaper to print so a publisher won't mutter about costs unless your book takes on epic proportions. This makes my theoretic answer a practical one as well: leave out the padding and keep only the quality material you *truly* need. Quality, not length is what keeps readers going or turns them off. My own novels are short because, while the plots are fairly complex, the overall pace is brisk and the style condensed. If my plots allowed digression or a slower pace was needed, I wouldn't hesitate to make my novels much longer.

If writing to length is important anywhere it's in the relative length of scenes (which keeps your pacing on track) and the planning of chapters. Most novels for young readers are highly episodic. I try to write chapters that can be read in one sitting, tell a complete story, establish a link to the next chapter, and lay some groundwork for the book's conclusion. With my plots and style this takes 3500-4500 words; yours might be quite different.

How Do You Hook Your Reader?

Theoretic answer: with a pleasurable and rewarding story.

Practical answer: with a strong plot. The best hook of all is a problem interesting enough to make you stick it out till the solution.

With believable characters. The best plots spring from the combination of character and circumstance. If we don't care about the characters, we don't care about the problem.

By combining the surprising with the predictable. Make your readers feel smart; let them see something a character doesn't. It will heighten the surprise of a plot twist afterwards, and then they'll have to see what happens next. Play fair though: don't drag in some never-before-mentioned wealthy aunt on the last page.

With varied tone and pacing. Something sad or suspenseful makes the funny parts funnier, and vice versa. A reflective passage heightens the impact of the next action sequence. Short establishing and transition sequences allow more attention to be focussed on important scenes of greater length.

By writing so clearly your readers are never intimidated. Reading is hard work; why make it harder? This doesn't mean they'll never need a dictionary to read you. A clear style inspires trust enough to know that a difficult word is worth looking up, and not just a pointless stumbling block some "smart" adult has stuck in.

With a memorable title and an attractive book. No matter how good the story, you have to get somebody to look at it first, which means titles are important. So important, in fact, that everybody will have a better idea than yours, particularly your publisher.

Publishers usually control titles and always control book design. They might be brilliant, but don't substitute blind faith for your own common sense, because that's all marketing savvy boils down to. Good publishers will never hesitate to answer your questions, explain their reasons, and tell you to take it or leave it. At first. Later you'll have a say. When you're despairing about it all at three in the morning just remember that they liked your invitation and now they're passing it around. See you at the party.

* Books are made by printing many pages at once on both sides of large sheets called signatures, which are then folded down to book size, cut, and bound. If you fold a sheet of paper four times alternating from the top and side, then cut all the folds but the spine, you'll find you have thirty-two pages.

3

Writing for Juveniles

Introduction

The years between eight and twelve reveal the individualization of both the interests and the abilities of the children. Although many readers have reached a level of independence, others still require a great range of materials to read and to listen to. Often the pressure of the peer group may determine reading choices. The perceptions and views built up with the literature can give children a strong affective and cognitive basis for life and a secure ground in literacy. And children in the fourth or fifth grade require books at their interest level, while written at a level that they can handle. They need books they can become immersed in so that they feel the satisfaction and pleasure that a book can give. Books written with a controlled vocabulary but little art seldom make a child want to do any reading.

Children in the middle years are gaining reading power through in-depth experience with novels. They enjoy reading several books by a favourite author, or a series of books about a familiar set of characters. Common themes link the most widely read books—humour, school friends, mystery and fantasy. Boys and girls may prefer different types of books, yet there are fine novels which, if brought to their attention, will fill the needs of both and present non-sexist portrayals.

Children who have developed into mature independent readers in the middle years need to deepen their reading experiences by moving into quality alongside quantity. Novels featuring other cultures or other contexts can present these young readers with problems and situations of greater complexity along with subtle characterization and multi-faceted plot structures. For many children, novels provide road maps for the difficulties of contemporary life.

Of course, over the years, such books as *The Hardy Boys* and *Nancy Drew* have remained popular with children. They enjoy the familiar plot structures and take comfort in the stock heroes that accompany the narrative. While children want a reality base in their books, they will accept stories set in other times, other cultures, other countries. This age group, even if reading fantasy, has to be able to identify with and put themselves in the context of the main characters of the story. Most publishers seem most interested in fiction. Realistic contemporary fiction with main characters that children can believe in and identify with—sport stories, horse stories, mysteries, adventures, fantasies, stories about peer relationships. Today books for children are a popular item. Professionals who delayed having children until their careers were established are now launching families and buying books. The juvenile market is the fastest growing in publishing today.

How I Do It

Jean Little

"How do you know how to do it?" a child asked me.

It sounded like a simple, straightforward question. When I tried to answer it, however, I found that it was so profound that I had no idea what to say. I believe it is the one question no good writer can answer. I have some inkling of how I do it, but how I know how remains mysterious. Yet here are a few pointers I have picked up from my reading of other people's books and a description of the process I go through when writing, rewriting and re-rewriting a novel.

These are not rules and, even if you take every hint I can offer, I do not promise that what you are writing will come to life. There are no guarantees in this line of work. There are no shortcuts either. Writing a novel may be absorbing and even, occasionally, joyous, but it is not easy.

The single, most important thing you can do to help yourself become an able writer is read. Good books are your first and best teachers. This may seem self-evident but not everyone seems to grasp how crucial it is for any writer to be on friendly terms with words. I do not mean that you should sit down and analyse, searching out theme, symbols and structure as though you were writing an essay for English class. When you want to get to know a person, you do not start by doing an autopsy. That way, you end up with a corpse instead of a friend. Read with loving attention, taking into yourself the rhythms, the quirkiness, the enticing, exciting possibilities in our language. Don't make notes. If you are any good, you will find your own writing voice. Deliberately imitating another writer's style is a sure way to produce a weak book.

Read the best. Read contemporary authors rather than concentrating only on the classics. Rudyard Kipling and E. Nesbit have a lot to teach a beginning writer, but what was written for children then, while it still makes wonderful reading, has an old-fashioned tone and portrays a world which is unfamiliar to modern children and unacceptable to today's editors. Look for the genre where you feel most at home but don't restrict yourself to it. If you still believe there is one right way to produce the perfect children's book, you have not read nearly enough.

If you are a Canadian, be sure to read the children's literature of this country, for it has its own sound and sense of place.

Whether or not you learn anything about the craft of writing from Book Immersion, you should enjoy yourself enormously. If you end up discouraged about your own ability, perhaps you needed discouraging. If you end up humbled but also excited, proceed to the next step.

Wait for a book to come to you asking to be written. This may stem from something you hear a child say, a memory of your own childhood, a twist of plot which intrigues you, a glimpse of a landscape in a fantasy world; it may be a combination of several of these or something entirely different. For me, almost always, it begins with a child and a question.

What if a child realized, after his father's death, that his mother's Christmas stocking holds nothing but an orange and a candy cane because his parents had always filled each other's stockings? Wondering what he would do led me to write *Mama's Going To Buy You A Mockingbird*.

Most novels begin with a writer's itch to explore the possibilities posed by such a question. This is the one time where inspiration plays an important part. Don't even start unless you are really eager to know the place or the character or the situation better. During the long months you will have to spend wrestling with this book, you will have many moments, days, weeks when you will loathe the thing. If you begin with a sermon you feel you ought to preach or a "relevant" topic you imagine may sell, you will never make it through or, if you do, the book will be a lacklustre effort.

So you're inspired. What next? There is no one right way to begin. Some authors start by doing research for a year or two. Some work out elaborate plots. I begin by writing chapter one.

I cannot plan anything until I get to know the people. I have to hear them talking, follow them around awhile. As I write these opening pages, I know that I will be rewriting them many times before the book is done. When I wrote *Kate*, I counted. I revised the first chapter twenty-five times.

I love writing beginnings though. I start the story at a point of tension or change. I never start with the main character cosily waking up to another sunny morning. He or she is usually puzzled, afraid, irritated or sad. The first sentence should pull the reader right into the thick of things. It should leave that reader wondering why? or who? or what next?

Sal Copeland was scared.

Mine For Keeps

James had wet the bed again.

Take Wing

The door would not open.

Look Through My Window

"You can't climb up here," Marilyn Dickson said. "You're not allowed."

Little By Little

It does not have to be dramatic, witty or full of information. It only has to make the reader want to continue reading. The second sentence is, after all, as important as the first. I try to make the opening chapter lively and full of feelings children instantly recognize. I do not introduce the whole cast of characters in one long descriptive paragraph. The information might be useful but it is not emotionally engaging. I usually bring the people in when they have a part to play in the story. Once in awhile, a major character is physically absent early in the book for some reason. In that case, I pique the heroine's and the reader's curiosity by circulating rumours about this soon-to-be-important person.

I try to reveal the thoughts and emotions of my characters through what they say and do, their silences, their shrugs. When you are watching television, nobody stops the story to say, "Laura is feeling unhappy." You see her misery in the droop of her shoulders and hear it in her glum speech. It is hard not to explain everything but you should assume your reader is perceptive. Even babies read body language accurately. This cannot be overemphasized. Don't tell too much: show it instead.

When you write, you also have to decide from whose point of view you are writing. I did not think this through until I was working on my second novel *Home From Far*. There the point of view switches back and forth between Jenny and Michael. I soon found that I could not interject more than a quick sentence or two of Michael's thoughts when I was seeing things through Jenny's consciousness. It is obvious, of course, when you are writing in the first person that the main character is the person interpreting everything. But this can be equally true in a story told in the third person but through a single viewpoint. Whatever you decide, be consistent.

I personally feel that younger children, under the age of twelve perhaps, prefer stories told from a single viewpoint and in the third person. They are apt to identify completely with the main character and will even skip bits which leave him or her out. Many authors write for teenagers wholly in introspective first person but I believe they may be more challenged by a book told from two or three vantage points. Beware though of too many protagonists. This can lead to confusion and rob your story of its power.

An interesting decision you must make, if you write a book in the first person, is whether or not the person telling the story knows it all or only part of it. Also you may want to indicate what made him or her decide to write it down. This is not necessary. Jane Eyre never explains to her dear reader what has prompted her to tell all.

Authors often make these decisions unconsciously. When I began to write *Kate*, she took over from the first. The more experienced you become, the more you see what it is you are doing, but if the story you are telling is powerful, it will usually arrive with its own shape. Writers do make false starts, however, and have to begin again. I heard Betsy Byars say that once she was on her way to post a finished manuscript when she realized it was told from the wrong point of view. She turned around, went home, and rewrote the book. This is an extreme example but you are a second-rate writer if you put your longing to be done with the task ahead of the demands made on you by the story. The book is not finished until it is the best you can do.

When I first started working with Ellen Rudin, she sent me a book which I find invaluable: *The Elements of Style* by William Strunk Jr., published by Macmillan and edited and added to by E.B. White. It is a small book but it will help you to clean up your prose. Ellen was one smart editor.

Avoid depending on adverbs or adjectives to do what is better left to nouns and verbs. I often use adverbs in a quick first draft to act as signposts to myself during revision. I only leave them in later if I am unable to say what I want without them. Eschew qualifying words such as *quite, very, rather, just, sort of* and *kind of. Suddenly* is also a word which is almost irresistible and usually extraneous. Whether or not you use a computer, remember that the urge to insert can be fatal while the strength to delete is what separates the good writers from the mediocre ones. A book that demonstrates this beautifully is *Sarah Plain and Tall* by Patricia MacLachlan. No wonder she won the Newbery Medal for it. So much feeling in so few words.

Have the children in the story play significant roles in the resolution of the plot. Never have some adult march in and settle everything.

Try to make the minor characters believable but do not let them shove your hero or heroine into the sidelines. Since we ourselves are adults, sometimes our sympathy is with the parents and, before we know it, we are writing a book about grown-up problems. Children occasionally have flashes of insight into their elders but not often. Why should they? They have problems of their own. Don't use the book to try to explain us to them.

When Jeremy's father died in *Mama's Going To Buy You A Mockingbird*, I knew that the mother's grief would be more overwhelming than my portrayal of it showed. But I was writing Jeremy's story, not hers. Although I personally grieved with her, I could not let it become the focus of the book.

When you have finished a chapter, read it aloud and you will hear false notes your eyes have missed. Have someone else read it aloud and you will squirm but you will be made aware of additional weak spots.

Never make up your mind that something you have written is perfect. It will only hurt more when it becomes necessary to cut it. Keep the health of the story in mind rather than brooding over how many drafts you've done and how unreasonable your editor is.

A fine editor is a writer's best friend. After I had worked on *Mama's Going To Buy You A Mockingbird* for a couple of years, my editor suggested that I delete Jeremy's four-year-old sister. She was so cute. I was fond of her. But, when I looked to see what part she really played in the novel, I discovered she said only two things that mattered and was always in the way. Exit Caroline. It was a wrench, at the time, but now I cannot imagine her as part of the Talbot family. I would never have seen she was merely cluttering up my book if my editor had not courageously pointed it out.

Occasionally editors are wrong, however. The trick is to be able to distinguish which of their suggestions are inspirations and which are merely wrongheaded. They have the same difficulty with us, of course. The writer-editor relationship is demanding, sometimes infuriating, but when it is good, wonderful books result. Always, even if you are quite sure you are right, let some time go by before you prepare to do battle. It may be that the editor knows something is wrong but is proposing a poor solution. After all, if the careful editor has missed your point, what chance does the poor reader have? Don't merely react: think.

If you believe, from the first page to the last, that you have written a masterpiece, you haven't. If, on the other hand, you are sunk in gloom, convinced that every word you have written or ever will write is worthless, be of good cheer. That is normal. We have all felt that. Try this test. Actually pitch the whole thing into the wastebasket. Can you now walk away and leave it there? Then perhaps you are not a writer. You are that even more important person, an observant and appreciative reader. Great. We need lots more of those.

But you are sneaking that hated manuscript out of the basket. There is, you discover, a spark somewhere in all those ashes, a character crying out to be given a chance at life. Good. Go to the rescue. Start working. Writing is hard work. Joyous, absorbing, frustrating, exciting, soul-satisfying, lovely, hard work. Worth doing well. Best of luck.

Getting Started

Bernice Thurman Hunter

"How do I get started?" This is the question I am most often asked. Well, like most authors, I have loved writing since early childhood. In school I soon discovered that "composition" was my favourite subject; a thrill ran up my spine when I was handed a long, lined piece of foolscap. A blank page meant to me "write something," even as a blank page begs an artist to "draw something."

I began my writing career with short stories and articles. Actually, my first published book, *That Scatterbrain Booky* (Boo-key), came about by accident. One awful day I fell victim to that horrible disease, that author's nightmare, "writer's block." Then, almost instantly, I had the reverse experience—an inspiration. Lots of interesting things happened when I was a kid, I thought, so why not write about them?

I decided to begin with an exciting and traumatic incident in my childhood. The great event was the birth of my baby brother. He was born at home, in the middle bedroom, in the middle of the night. I was ten years old, just the right age to be thrilled with a new baby in the family, and not so young as to be jealous of it.

I began to write feverishly, and as I wrote one memory triggered another and that memory triggered another and soon I had about one hundred scribbled pages. (I still write, initially, in longhand because my pen gives me a chance to ponder; the word processor has to wait.) By this time I realized I had not a short story, but the beginnings of a book.

This book also made me aware of the fact that the past held more fascination for me than the present or the future, and that truth is often stranger than fiction—and funnier too! But recreating the past demands lots of research. I could not depend entirely upon my memory or my imagination. (Make a mistake and for sure your sin will find you out!) So I prowled about the archives, especially the City of Toronto's and Eaton's; I pored over old newspapers at the Reference Library; I haunted several historical societies; I picked the brains of relatives (some even older than me!); I sought out old friends and ran up long-distance telephone bills tracking them down; I watched ancient films on television (thanks to Elwy Yost); questing, questing, questing.

But, in the final analysis, it was my own memory-bank—that

amazing God-given computer between my ears—that enabled me to relive and recapture the past. Little details popped unexpectedly into my head, often triggered by sounds and sights and smells, bringing back to me the settings and feelings of the "olden days" (as my grandchildren would so graciously put it).

Recently a fourteen-year-old aspiring writer asked me how I knew enough about pioneer life to write *Lamplighter*, a story set in Muskoka one hundred years ago. The answer is simple. When my father was an elderly man, living in a nursing home, he was typically forgetful. "Nobody's been to see me in three weeks," he'd complain. (I knew my sister had been there the day before.) Well, Dad may not have been able to remember yesterday, or what he'd just had for lunch, ("They didn't give me a bite to eat today. I don't know what I'm paying for.") but he could vividly recall his childhood.

So I began to ply him with questions (the past gave us something wonderful to talk about and share) and my eager interrogation unlocked his dormant memories. Each day our visits became fascinating journeys backwards in time. Stories, anecdotes, folklore, family traditions, came pouring forth and I began to write them down. I often forgot my notebook and would resort to anything at hand: envelopes, paper serviettes, matchbook covers, the backs of business cards; once I even had to use the palm of my hand! Wouldn't you think I could have remembered the scratch pad that most authors wouldn't be caught dead without?

Several years went by, after my father died, and I was so busy with *Booky* and *Margaret* that I completely forgot the scraps of paper until one day, while cleaning a clothes-closet (a rare occurrence), I came across a Loblaws bag full of something "scrunchy." Curious, I held the bag upside-down and shook out upon the floor—my dad's memories. I began reading the scribbled reminders and as I read excitement mounted. I shuffled the flurry of crumpled bits and pieces around like a jigsaw puzzle and gradually, out of the chaos, a word-picture began to emerge. Right then I started a list and eventually I had some semblance of order.

Then I launched a search into Dad's old box of "stuff" that I had neglected to throw out . . . and I found treasures. What a thrill to discover a diary, yellow and crackling with age, and a nineteenth-century autograph book which had belonged to my dad's sisters one hundred years ago. Voilà . . . *Lamplighter* was born.

Another question I hear a lot is, "How do you write so convincingly of childhood?" Once again, the answer is easy, or so it seems to me.

I simply become the child in the story. I sometimes say that I feel as if I'm stuck-in-gear at about twelve years of age. Either that or I just never quite grew up. I guess I am still a child at heart.

For years I worked alone and shared my thoughts with no one. And that got me exactly nowhere. One day I was crying the blues to another writer, a successful poet, and she said, "Why don't you join a workshop?" I said, "What's a workshop?" Appalled at my ignorance she told me that writing alone was like working in a vacuum. What I needed was feedback and constructive criticism. So she invited me to a workshop she belonged to, a group of writers with varying degrees of success, but all committed to producing good literature for children. I had never read out loud to anyone before, so with quaking voice I began the first chapter of *That Scatterbrain Booky* and their enthusiastic reception of my work, and their steadfast encouragement, was just the incentive I needed. I discovered then and there that a good workshop is absolutely priceless.

Next came membership in CANSCAIP (Canadian Society of Children's Authors, Illustrators and Performers), a wonderful conglomeration of childrens' authors, illustrators and performers who offer solace in defeat and applause in victory. And much, much more.

It is also my good fortune to be invited to schools and libraries across Canada to talk to children about my life and work. They are amazingly interested in the past and very candid in their response. I listen avidly to everything they have to say. They are at once my best and worst critics; they are totally honest and wonderfully naive. They make me wish I was a child again (just for tonight!) so I could start from scratch and never waste a minute of that precious time—childhood. "We get too soon old and too late smart."

Although my books are categorized as fiction, to begin I must have a basis of truth. I guess I am a "realist" because I draw most of my characters from life. People who know me well, my family, cousins, old friends, usually recognize the characters and locales of my stories no matter how hard I try to camouflage them. So I have to be careful what I say!

I like to encourage people to write about themselves, about things they know and experiences they have lived. One time, months after giving this advice, I received a letter from a girl saying, "I started to write about the day my dad brought home our dog and everything you said came true. That memory triggered another memory and that memory triggered another one, and pretty soon I was writing as fast as my hand would go."

There was a P.S. at the end of that letter which warmed the cockles of my heart. "My teacher said it was the best story he'd ever read and he gave me an A+. Do you think that means I am destined to be a writer like you when I grow up?" I wrote back and answered "YES!" (I think I'll frame that letter.)

Another thing I'd like to stress is that you are never too young or too old to write. I was fifty when I published my first article, and fifty-nine when my first book came out. A writer I know at the other end of the scale published his first book at the tender age of fourteen. Authorship is obviously no respecter of age. If you believe in yourself, and never give up, you will succeed.

Remember, a story begins with a single word, just as a marathon begins with a single step.

Writing Humorous Stories

Ken Roberts

Annette Curtis Klause, a librarian in Maryland, writes "Children have a different sense of humour from adults. I know this—they laugh at my jokes. Try telling an adult that all the magic books have disappeared—you'll see."

She's right. In part, that different sense of humour comes from an emerging understanding of language. Puns are funny. Spoonerisms are hilarious. Word play and coincidence are both sources of great amusement.

It is always hard to write about humour, even harder when it's humour for young people. Perhaps it's best to start with a joke.

Nancy and Jo-Anne were walking down the street. "I have a joke," said Jo-Anne. "A bricklayer always knew exactly how many bricks each job needed. He never missed. One day, after finishing a wall, he backed up and tripped over an extra brick. Furious he picked up the brick and guess what he did with it?"

"I don't know," said Nancy.

"He threw it in the air."

Jo-Anne waited for Nancy to laugh. Nancy didn't laugh. She frowned. "Here's another one," said Jo-Anne quickly. "There was this couple. The woman had a poodle. The man smoked cigars. He hated her poodle. She hated his cigars. They went on vacation. The poodle and cigars went too.

"In the car, the man said, 'Get rid of that poodle.' 'Get rid of that cigar,' the woman snarled back. In their train compartment the man said, 'Get rid of that poodle.' 'Get rid of that cigar,' the woman snarled again. In their airplane the man said 'Get rid of that poodle.' 'Get rid of that cigar,' the woman hissed. 'O.K.' said the man. 'All right,' agreed the woman.

"So they each opened their windows, counted to three, and threw out the poodle and the cigar at exactly the same instant. The poodle landed on the wing of the plane, and guess what was in his mouth?"

"The cigar," said Nancy.

"No. The brick," said Jo-Anne, and the two friends laughed.

As individual stories, neither tale is remotely funny. Together, they are. They rely, as does much of humour, on surprise and repetition. I laughed when I heard the joke because I had forgotten about the stupid brick. Many humorous writers rely on the fact that almost forgotten events, twisted and suddenly reincorporated into a story, cause people to laugh in sudden recognition. Listen to people you think are funny and you'll find they are probably good listeners who store away tidbits of conversation to throw back later.

A third basic element of humour is anticipation. A great deal of visual humour milks an audience's delight in knowing something in advance. Clowns are fond of looking for each other while walking backwards, just missing collision after collision while the audience howls. This type of humour is the reverse of surprise. It is the expectation of surprise in someone else.

Let's say that just after telling her brick joke, Jo-Anne leaves and Jack comes along. Jack says, "Hey Nancy, Jo-Anne just told me this wonderful joke. See, there was this bricklayer . . ." Nancy smiles to herself and lets Jack continue. Nancy has a secret. She knows that when Jack gets to the end and asks, "And guess what was in his mouth?" she can say "The brick, of course," and turn the joke into one on Jack. If this scene were setup in a story the reader, like Nancy, could laugh in expectation of what will happen.

Oddly enough, the only form of writing which uses surprise, anticipation and repetition as frequently as humour is the horror story. A monstrous hand suddenly crashes through a wall and causes the reader to gasp. That's surprise. There's a dark hallway into which victims continually vanish. That's repetition. The hero decides to walk down that same hallway. That's anticipation.

Humour and horror stories share one other trait. Both commonly take place in worlds which resemble the "normal" world but are on a slight tilt. The tilt of horror stories is easily recognized. Magic, sorcery, and an acceptance of ghosts are standard symbols which allow us to suspend disbelief when reading horror stories. Much of humour works the same. Daniel Pinkwater's *Hoboken Chicken Emergency* assumes a world in which the police chase a giant chicken. Since this is not normal practice, Pinkwater papers his "Hoboken" with people who are odd. Then we can accept them doing bizarre things.

Although humour and horror rely on similar techniques to get at different emotions, the structure of comic novels is often different. Horror stories are almost invariably plot-driven. Humour stories can be plot-driven, character-driven, or some combination of the two.

Character-driven humour derives its comedy from figuring out how certain well-defined characters will behave when faced with a particular dilemma. Robert Newton Peck's Soup series, Beverley Cleary's Ramona books, and Helen Cresswell's Bagthorpe saga are all character-driven. The cast is the same, book after book, but they face different situations.

Plot-driven humour follows a comic idea instead of the characters themselves. Most of Gordon Korman's books are plot-driven. Thomas Rockwell's *How To Eat Fried Worms* is plot-driven. The distinction is easy to spot. Watch three episodes of "Three's Company," and you will probably see three variations of the same plot; a misunderstanding leads to a lie which causes complications. Watch three episodes of "M*A*S*H," and you'll see an emphasis on following set characters through problems. The difference, while substantial, does not mean that plot-driven humour has dull characters or that character-driven humour has no plot.

Here is one last common element in much of humorous writing. The more broad and off-beat characters and plot become, the more they need some base in sanity. Comedy duos almost always feature a straight-man and a "character." The straight-man helps us relax. A cast of pure "characters" is incredibly difficult to control. We shake our heads and want to scream "This is nuts." With a straight, normal central character, we can focus on strange events from a position of safety; we can focus. The title character of Robert McCloskey's *Homer Price* is a straight, normal boy with whom dozens of "characters" interact. Helen Cresswell's Jack, of the Bagthorpe saga, is described as being ordinary in every way, and he is surrounded by a family of crazy people. Without Jack, the stories would have no direction.

The best way to understand these elements, and others, is to read humour for young people. You will, at times, think the most popular books somewhat sophomoric in their use of simple word play and coincidence. Remember that young people really do have a different sense of humour (anyone with a nine-year-old who has discovered joke books can attest to this).

I was just staring out the window trying to think of an ending and guess what fell from the sky. A cigar!

Developing a Series

Eric Wilson

Before I became a writer it looked easy. Therefore I made every possible mistake.

Except one.

I always believed in what I wanted to do: write books for my own grade eight students, the ones who hated books. I took almost a year, working after school, to write a story about a grade eight boy with a poor self-image and a tyrannical father. The kid ran away from home and got tangled in the drug culture of Vancouver. Eventually he went home, definitely sadder and possibly wiser.

"Someone I know wrote this," I said nervously to my class. "He wants to know that you think of it."

"Do we have to do a book report?"

"No."

"Okay."

I sat on the edge of my desk. Cleared my throat. Swallowed. "Um . . ." Another swallow, then I read the opening sentence: "Underarm pollution."

"I don't believe it!" The boy nearest my desk ran forward. "Hey, it does say that!" Others joined him to stare at the manuscript, and then a boy in the corner turned from staring out the window. "So," he said, releasing a theatrical yawn, "what happens next?"

For the next five years, as I heard all the reasons why publishers didn't want my manuscripts, I remembered that first class and continued to believe in my words. Meanwhile, of course, I made mistakes. Despite constantly haranguing my students to plan their stories, I made up my books as I wrote them. I didn't study the work of successful authors writing for this market. I didn't read books on the subject. But I kept trying, eventually learned my lessons and broke into print with *Murder on the Canadian* (happily, the book survives and so does the train, aboard which I am writing these comments while en route between school visits in British Columbia and Alberta).

Success at last, after years of frustration but never a lack of determination or belief in myself. It was May 5, 1975, that I rode the London Underground to the office of Margaret Clark, children's editor at The Bodley Head publishers, and heard the good news that at last I would be published. I still have the newspaper I was reading on the way to her office.

When Margaret asked if I'd write a second Tom Austen Mystery for them, there was no chance I'd refuse. Then a third book appeared, followed by a fourth in which I introduced Tom's sister, Liz. At first her character was based on a close friend but quickly Liz Austen, like Tom, became a very real person to me in her own right.

Meanwhile a few letters arrived from kids who were enjoying my books. A girl in England was the first to write, followed by one in Ontario who swore she was my number one fan "even though I bet you've got hundreds of others." Could that be, I wondered? After all, my reviews had been mostly unpleasant and one professor of library science had even demanded that her students have nothing to do with *Murder on the Canadian*.

Then a boy told me he'd read the book four times and another claimed nine readings. I was invited to a Vancouver school as a speaker and nervously faced a gym full of kids. Later I was introduced to a girl who'd received special permission to travel across the city to hear me speak; that moment was a major turning point in my life. My confidence became stronger and I developed a thick enough hide to continue writing despite a fair degree of hostility from the critics, happily balanced by growing approval and support from other adults.

I continued to write about Tom and Liz Austen because they'd become important to me and to my readers. They were familiar figures who could take the reader to both the exotic outposts of our country and the familiar landmarks. Then, with a book about a hostage-taking at Disneyland, I took my first real step into issues. Latin America: why are people fighting there? The Dragon: what kind of person is a terrorist? Cody: can courage take a police officer beyond the call of duty? These issues I addressed in the book, hoping they would provoke thought and discussion even though the book was essentially a fast-paced adventure.

As each new book appeared I read the reviews and tried to learn from them. I listened to my editors and profited from their advice. But mostly I listened to the kids, learning from their feedback on earlier books and seeking their ideas for the future.

After I became an author for Collins, a company that has backed me with faith and financial resources, I showed them the manuscript of an earlier book, a novel rather than a mystery. By now I had enough of a readership that Collins was interested even though Tom and Liz Austen were not in this story; I went to work on a rewrite with the help

of Shelley Tanaka, an excellent Toronto editor, who helped me introduce a mystery element while retaining my focus on the strengths,
laughter, fears and especially the courage of disabled kids attending a
summer camp in Saskatchewan. Although some letters expressed dismay that I'd ignored the Austens with this book, most readers reacted
favourably and *Summer of Discovery* has become one of my most
popular stories.

I've since written one more book without Tom and Liz, *The
Unmasking of 'Ksan*, the story of a sixteen-year-old who is dealing
with the loss of his mother while joining with an Indian girl in the
search for a ceremonial mask, a device which enabled me to explore the
culture of the Gitksan people of northern British Columbia. I have in
mind other issue-oriented books that will not involve Tom and Liz, but
I'm fully aware that the series about the Austens will always be my
most popular books because series books are comfortable to the reader. Therefore in my newest Tom and Liz adventure, *Code Red at the
Supermall*, I've involved them in some personal issues: Tom witnesses
a racist attack that he feels powerless to combat, and Liz also faces a
difficult situation when she dates a boy who makes demands of her.

How do I write a book? The first step involves selecting a location
and then living there for about two months. During this time I scout
possible settings for individual scenes, read local history, talk to
people, get a sense of the community.

Back home in Victoria I spend a couple of months carefully planning my story and making detailed notes about the major characters:
place of birth, relationship with others, ambitions, fears and dreams,
etc. I write a thirty-page plot outline for my editor, digest her comments, and then break down every scene into the events that will occur,
what I will reveal about my characters in the scene, what setting details
I want to incorporate and the clues and red herrings I will use.

When I'm writing my story I force myself to complete five pages
before I have lunch, then I revise and retype. Still to come, after the
first draft is finished, are the consultations with my editor and also a
meeting with the most important people of all: kids. I arrange with a
Victoria school for the manuscript to be read by about eight kids, each
of whom keeps a chapter-by-chapter journal with thoughts and suggestions. Then I meet with the kids and make changes based on their ideas.

In summary, there are no definitive rules for the writer attempting
a series for children. Stay with the familiar, yet introduce the exotic,
tell a good story, yet challenge with thought-provoking topics . . . and
mostly believe in yourself and persevere.

Writing Mystery Stories

Marion Crook

Many of you will remember your introduction to mysteries, curled up in an armchair, hiding from the family chores, engrossed in *Nancy Drew* or *The Hardy Boys,* enthralled by their world of excitement and adventure. The present generation of young readers has a much wider choice of titles and authors, but they still want to experience the action and excitement of a mystery, the thrill of suspense, the anxiety of not knowing how the hero will survive, the confidence that somehow he will extricate himself once again.

Young readers still expect you to write a story that unfolds in a logical, rational manner. They want a "detecting puzzle" with an ending that satisfies. They want a story where the questions the author raises are answered, and the hero triumphs.

This enthusiastic, voracious group of readers demands good plots with adventures, sharp dialogue with some humour, and an emotional problem that tugs at their feelings. As a mystery writer you must be facile with your craft yet still be able to create excitement with an almost electric personality that sparks throughout the story. Craft alone does not stimulate young readers. They respond directly to the communication of eagerness and excitement from the mind of the author. It is that indefinable aspect of your personality, your own magic, that the reader grabs from the pages of your book. How you, the writer, breathe this energy into the story is your art, something you develop in yourself. From books, from lectures, you can learn about the craft of writing mysteries and learn to shape your energies with some skills used by other writers. I have picked some guidelines to storytelling that may help you direct your ideas. These "rules" are not unbreakable. You may well write an intriguing story ignoring every one of them, but I have found that they help me.

The reader must be convinced that the villain is capable of hurting the hero. The more powerful the villain, the greater the threat to our hero. Because the hero is someone who will be tested, the antagonist in a mystery needs to be an individual of some power. He or she often has an overriding need that oozes forth from a character fault. Many of my villains seem to pick over the seven deadly sins and choose greed. Once the villain is committed to a certain greed, all reprehensible actions seem reasonable.

Humour should bubble through the plot occasionally. Young readers want suspense, but they want humour to act as a release from tension, allowing them to settle comfortably into the story before tension increases.

Yet your mystery must maintain suspense, a kind of impelling anxiety created in the reader. It is impossible to build suspense if the reader does not care about the hero. The reader must identify emotionally with the hero, must like or admire him and feel that he is vulnerable to the threat of the villain. The reader needs this process of identification in order to be anxious about the hero's future and to be absorbed by the suspense.

The characters in your story make the action real to the reader. If the reader identifies with the character, the story becomes important. Your character should be so real to you, the author, that you know her reactions in almost any situation.

I find my main character is more interesting to me if she is an independent thinker, a little different from her family, and friends. I also like her to be physically mobile. She needs to be able to move around in her environment with some ease. In *Crosscurrents* Megan rides a tug boat into the action of the story. In *Stone Dead* Susan goes from ranch to ranch on her motor bike. I find a mobile protagonist is able to put herself into different settings, adding impetus to the story and allowing her to gather new information.

Young readers like to read from one person's point of view, preferably the protagonist's. Flashbacks are difficult for young readers, as are multiple points of view. While writing in the first person is the best way to keep religiously to one point of view, juvenile readers don't like first person narrative. They have difficulty separating the author from the fictional character telling the story. This was clear to me when my nine-year-old son told me after reading *Payment in Death*, "You're telling a lot of lies, you know, Mom. You never did all those things."

The setting helps define the characters. If your hero lives in a bedroom with rock-star posters, an elaborate stereo set and expensive musical equipment, the readers form an idea of his lifestyle, likes and dislikes. If he lives in a ranch house sharing a room with two brothers surrounded by lariats, cowboy boots and 4-H manuals, readers get a different sense of what he is like.

Readers of juvenile fiction like to go where they wouldn't be allowed to go in real life. In *Crosscurrents* Megan works with her uncle on his tug on the Fraser River. In *Hidden Gold Mystery* her father takes her up on his DC3 cat tractor. The setting—the tug, the cat tractor—help to define Megan as adventurous.

Settings can also enhance a mood. I find that readers do feel more suspense when the protagonist is out in the night. For one thing, a young protagonist is not supposed to be out at night. The fear of getting caught adds to the fear of the unknown. A night setting increases tension in a story as do abandoned houses, dark caves, attics, cellars, "rough" neighbourhoods and locked buildings—the school after dark in Claire Mackay's *The Minerva Program*. Any setting that emphasizes danger increases tension—the dangerous seas in *The Baitchopper* by Silver Donald Cameron.

The plot affects the suspense, the tension increasing and decreasing with plot development. It is sometimes difficult for a writer to judge the suspense of the story since he knows the outcome or knows, at least, the direction in which the story is going. A reader can give you a more objective view. When I am in danger of being submerged by my plots and subplots and I find myself grabbing for a maxim that can help me out of my difficulties, I use: If you can make the situation worse, do so. It seems somehow that by making things worse for the protagonist, I make things better for the story.

Young readers want the action of the plot to be absorbing. They particularly want action at the beginning of the book. One librarian told me that if something exciting doesn't happen in the first four pages, most young readers will bring the book back.

In *Hidden Gold Mystery*, Megan's pig gets into her mother's garden. Her mother threatens to kill it.

In *Crosscurrents*, on the first page, Grandma threatens to send Megan home.

In *Stone Dead*, Evelyn reports a bear in the meadow and Susan doesn't know how to get rid of it.

Young readers want new information or a new element of suspense introduced at the end of each chapter. They need it to encourage them to go on reading.

Writers hold a traditional pact with mystery readers. They agree to write an exciting story, with action, in which justice (some kind of justice) prevails and the protagonist triumphs. The reader expects to feel satisfied at the end of the story that all the important subplots have been resolved and the main problem solved.

The main problem must be interesting to the reader. Nine- to twelve-year-olds aren't usually fascinated by the world monetary system, so a plot that involves the world monetary system is unlikely to captivate them. Luckily young readers are interested in many things: computers, cars, fires, theft, embezzlement, murder. The problem must be of interest to the readers and important to the protagonist. While readers are interested in theft, they would be less interested in theft of stock from the bank than they would be in a rash of bicycle thefts. Bicycle thefts might affect the protagonist directly and cause direct, personal problems for her.

The problem should matter in the life of the protagonist. The problem should also have a time limit. It must be solved before her parents return, before school starts, before midnight.

The problem must also be difficult for the protagonist to solve. She must try the reasonable avenues, but the reader must not be able to see the solution clearly. The solution unfolds or comes to light with the development of the plot.

I try to leave my protagonist with as little support as possible. It isn't reasonable to suppose a child of say eleven would be without parental support. But it is possible to allow that situation to be temporary. Her parents are on vacation and the care-givers are emotionally distant, or uncaring, or busy. The protagonist can be accidentally without support as a result of a flood which isolates him on an island, or he misses the last ferry, or he is lost in the woods. Emotional and physical abandonment make him more vulnerable and the threats against him more likely.

When you create a world for the young, whether it is the world of a tugboat, a ranch, a grocery store or a school, be sure that you create a world as credible as possible. If the tugboaters call the cables they use "towlines," be sure you call them "towlines." If the ranch raises cattle, be sure you know an Angus from a Shorthorn. While readers understand that the story is fiction, they assume that the details are true. In some way you are responsible for an expansion of the reader's knowledge, and so have an obligation to be accurate.

The test of your writing is reading to young listeners. It can be exhilarating and humiliating. I have a grade five class in Vancouver who loyally listen to my early drafts. I can tell by their reactions— looking around, talking to their neighbours—when they are bored, and I can tell by their reactions—leaning forward, mouths open, eyes bright —when they are interested. If you read a portion of your mystery to a class of children and the story is interesting to them, they will ask you questions about what happens next. If they don't, they haven't been interested, and you need to rewrite. Young readers of mystery stories are enthusiastic, but they are also discriminating. They like your stories or they don't like them with equal ferocity. One of the best ways to test your appeal is to read to them—and listen to their response.

The world of young people continually changes. They respond to changing social pressures and move in and out of the world of children and the world of adults. You have to be always aware of what is shaping their lives right now, what is important to them today, what is interesting. When you write for young people, you must be prepared to never truly understand everything there is to know about their lives, to never truly be aware of all their current problems, to never be an "expert." You will always be learning from them.

Writing Short Stories

Jean Booker

I was once asked by a student which I preferred writing, the novel or the short story. My answer was that I enjoy both but I believe the short story is more challenging. For me, writing a novel is like painting a picture—the artist begins with a blank canvas then adds scenery or people, over a period of time, to make a final, complete picture. Writing a short story is more like taking a photograph—the photographer sees an interesting subject, decides which angle will make the best picture, then shoots to capture that particular moment.

If writing a short story is a challenge, then writing a short story for young people is even more of a challenge. Young people are very astute. The story must be interesting, not only to the reader but also to the writer. If the writer is enthusiastic about the subject, that enthusiasm will show and will keep the young reader turning the page. Young readers easily spot inconsistencies so research is important. If you are writing about antique cars you must know all about them. Children are very concerned with the sights, sounds and smells of their world and it is important to bring these things into your stories. Characters must be real so that the reader can identify with them. Plots must be interesting but not too complicated.

How can the writer put all these things into a story that is only fifteen hundred or two thousand words long? By keeping the writing tight and making every word count. This means that all aspects of the story must be intertwined and every word must move the story forward. My story, "Smokey," begins this way:

> Janice looked in dismay at her mother, "You don't mean it, we *can't* get rid of Smokey."
>
> Mrs. Dempster frowned, "Please don't be awkward Jan, you knew when you brought him home that pets weren't allowed in the apartment. You're just lucky the superintendent hasn't found out about him till now."

The dialogue not only introduces the heroine but also lets the reader know she's upset and why.

Young people are interested in many different things so it's easy to find ideas for short stories. Choose something you know, or would enjoy learning about. Ideas are everywhere. Ask the librarian at your public library—or at a nearby school—what kinds of stories children like to read, then read them. Subscribe to children's magazines and newspapers. Listen to children talking and watch them playing. Remember how you felt when you were eight or ten years old. If you find this difficult, look at some photographs of yourself when you were a child or listen to some of the music you liked then. Personal experiences, even dreams, can trigger story ideas—but beware—dreams that seem so vivid when you wake up can vanish by noon, so write them down. I keep a notebook by my bed and one in my purse, and I jot down story ideas whenever they come to me. I also keep a file of newspaper clippings which I hope will someday be used in stories. Other ideas can come from settings—a stormy lake or a spooky old house—or from characters you meet.

Characters are very important because they help the reader identify with the story, but a short story doesn't need a lot of characters. Two or three are all that are necessary and every one must have a reason for being in the story. Unlike the novel, where there is time to show all sides of a person, the good, the bad and the in-between, the short story only has room for one or two main character traits and those traits should be used to further the plot. For example, a girl who is alway poking her nose into other people's business solves a mystery because she's so curious. However, even though there isn't room in a short story for every single character trait the writer must know all about that person. If I can't see a character clearly in my mind I find it helps to write down everything about him—age, height, weight, colour of eyes, hair, even what makes him laugh, or cry.

As in any story, characters and plot are equally important and with stories for young people a plot works best if it has a short time span. A novel can tell the story of three generations in the life of a family, but to tell that same story in two thousand words or less would be impossible. An element of urgency also helps keep the story tight— the letter must be found by tomorrow or something dreadful will happen to the hero. I also find that planning the whole story before I begin to write it down helps keep the plot tight.

Most short stories for young people have a beginning, a middle and an end. The beginning of a story is very important because if the reader isn't hooked by the first few lines she won't read the rest— unlike a novel where the reader knows it takes the first few chapters to set the scene and introduce the characters. I find the best thing to do is to jump right in with both feet and I try to get as much information into the first paragraph as possible. I picture the opening scene in my mind then try to incorporate actions and feelings that will move the story forward. This is easier if you try to show the reader what is happening rather than tell him. For example, in my story, "Break In," instead of writing "Linda was cold and she was late for dinner," I wrote:

> Linda shivered and pulled her coat collar up against the
> wind. She looked at her watch. "We're going to be late
> for dinner again, Susie. Come on, let's run."

As well as having an interesting beginning, stories for young people should keep the reader's interest through the middle, which in turn should lead to the exciting conclusion. The middle usually tells how the heroine attempts to solve her problems—each attempt getting her into more trouble until she's faced with the worst problem possible and has to solve it or suffer the consequences. In the short story, two or three minor setbacks are all that are necessary before the heroine has to tackle the big one. In a well-plotted story, the problem solving should work on two levels. For example, in my story, "Julie," Julie has to paddle the canoe across the lake in a storm to get help for a man who is bleeding to death, but not only is she fighting the storm, she's fighting her fear of paddling the canoe alone because the last time she tried, she got stuck on a rock and looked foolish. A story for young people will always be more effective if the main character solves his own problem and doesn't get someone else—parents or teachers or friends—to do it for him. Once the problem is solved, the story is over and only a few sentences are needed to wrap things up.

After a story is written, I put it away for a while so that the next time I read it I can look at it objectively. Then I edit it. Editing means taking out every word that doesn't move the story forward, and it's not always easy, especially when there's a phrase or paragraph I think sounds good but really has nothing to do with the plot. In order to be ruthless about editing, it helps to think of the story as having been written by someone else, and yourself as an impartial reader. It also helps to read the story aloud to someone, or have someone else read it aloud to you. That way you can pick out words that are repeated too often or sentences that are awkward. At this stage I also check the length of the manuscript to make sure it meets the publisher's requirements. If you're not sure what a publisher is looking for, write and ask. Most magazines will send out writer's guidelines if you enclose a stamped addressed envelope. Marketing information can be found in newsletters put out by writing organizations such as CANSCAIP

(Canadian Society of Children's Authors, Illustrators and Performers) and The Canadian Authors Association. Unlike the novel, short stories can be sent out to several different publishers at the same time as long as they are marked "multiple submission." Seasonal stories should be sent out four months in advance.

Once your manuscript is in the mail forget about it. Take up the challenge and start another story. You'll find that writing short stories for young people is not only rewarding, it can also be fun.

Non-Fiction: Biographies

Meguido Zola

"At best, fact is harsh, recalcitrant matter, as tangible as the hunk of rusty iron one trips over and yet as shapeless as a paper hat in the rain. Fact is a cold stone, an inarticulate thing, dumb until something happens to it: and there is no use the biographer waiting for spontaneous combustion or miraculous alchemy. Fact must be rubbed up in the mind, placed in magnetic juxtaposition with other facts, until it begins to glow, to give off that radiance we call meaning. Fact is a biographer's only friend and worst enemy."

Paul Murray Kendall
The Art of Biography

"Biography is an illusion," claims British critic Margery Fisher, "a fiction in the guise of fact." That is to say, though the biographer is working with facts, he is ultimately calling upon the imagination—both his and the reader's—to breathe life into those facts. No less than the creator of fiction, therefore, the biographer is ultimately an artist, but, because facts are his stock-in-trade, he must be, in the words of writer Desmond McCarthy, "an artist upon oath."

Having written a number of children's biographies of contemporary Canadians—Terry Fox, Karen Kain, and Wayne Gretzky, to name a few—I have learned some useful things about working as "an artist upon oath."

I need to have a compelling reason to embark on the writing of a biography: only from this can commitment come. Let me give an example. Ever since an ambitious aunt entered me, at the age of four, into ballet school at the court of King Farouk of Egypt, I've had a fascination for the ballet. I've seen and admired most of the great ballerinas—Margot Fonteyn, Alicia Alonso, Cynthia Gregory, Natalia Makarova—but the dancing of Karen Kain has especially moved me in ways I will probably never comprehend. So to be offered the opportunity to write her life story was a summons I could not resist. Jane Yolen calls this "a tap on the shoulder"; and it was in response to it, she explains, that she wrote *Friend*, the biography of George Fox, convinced she had received a calling from the fiery founder of Quakerism himself.

My purpose in writing a biography is to show my subject as he or she really is or was. That might seem so obvious as not to need stating, unless one remembers that, until fairly recently, biography for children has been largely purposive: concerned, in the main, with the teaching and setting of examples, often with a consequent flagrant disregard for truth. As a thoughtful children's librarian has put it, commenting on Philip Guedalla's dictum that biography is a region bounded on its sides by history, fiction, obituary, and tedium: "If this is true, then in the region of children's biography we must add more points to our compass. On the northwest, hagiography: George with his little hatchet and Honest Abe gazing into the coals. On the northeast, didacticism: Helen Keller obscured by 'mists of adulation.' On the southwest, over-simplification: Einstein and his theory of relativity reduced to the third-grade reading level. On the southeast, propaganda: Crispus Attucks, a black hero of convenience. And from all directions, sentimentality, unwarranted fictionalization, lack of solid documentation, and distortion of history."

Little wonder there is a real paucity of good biography for children.

Showing my subject as he or she really is or was commits me, above all, to truth and authenticity—the touchstones of good biography. This is the work of the scholar. It means, for me, a good deal of painstaking labour, mostly in the form of first-hand research. For example, my biography of the children's entertainers Sharon, Lois and Bram entailed, among other things: reading up on all kinds of topics from the history of children's music in Canada to the theory of folk music arrangement; hours of interviews not only with the entertainers themselves but, also their audiences of children, and the teachers they work with in workshops; and attendance at public concerts, school performances and rehearsals, as well as composing sessions and planning meetings.

But the assembling of facts for a biography is only a beginning. I must now put the material together: select what is germane and significant; interpret and present it from a clear and coherent point of view; and shape the whole into a narrative—as distinct from a mere chronology—that has *meaning* for my intended reader. Here the sensitivity, insight and discriminating judgement of the artist are at a premium.

What is most crucial in this part of the process is finding a theme. Theme can never be imposed on the material, of course, but must arise organically from it. As Marchette Chute, who notes that she had to read some ten thousand books and papers before identifying the theme of her children's book on the life of Shakespeare, warns: "It is only too easy to decide on a thesis and then start looking for the material that will support it, but it is a method that never results in a good biography. The material must all be collected first, and if the work has been done properly the thesis will eventually emerge."

For example, what was the thread that, for me as his biographer, knit together the life of Terry Fox? Courage? Selflessness? Vision? I remember struggling with this question long and hard. The answer came to me, at last, when Betty Fox, his mother, said about him, "Terry is average in everything but determination." And it was reaffirmed in Terry's own words, which came back to me only after he had died and we were just beginning to understand something of his achievement: "Dreams are made if people try."

Some lives may never yield up their significance to the would-be biographer. This was the case for me in my attempt to put together a biography of teenage skating wonder Tracy Wainman. Drawing a blank, I was forced to abandon the project. Yet other lives may be too complex, or deal with ideas and issues too difficult to be written about within the comprehension of a young reader. Such was the realization that came to me more than halfway through my biography of Pierre Trudeau: that I could not fairly interpret the man's character—let alone the ideas and issues he had grappled with over a lifetime—for the sixth graders for whom the book had been commissioned. So, once again, I had to abandon a project for which I had already completed all the research.

As if creating an accurate and authentic portrait of my subject were not already demanding enough, I must, at the same time, present a portrait that is vivid and illuminating. I must bring my subject to life for the young reader. For if the man or woman I am writing about does not live in my pages, then, as Margery Fisher points out, "the child would do better to turn to an historical treatise or to fiction."

It is here, especially, that biography makes its demands on me as an artist. Clearly, the key is good writing. For me, this means at least two things: writing that from the first captures the reader's attention by its liveliness and immediacy; and writing that sustains the reader's interest as it gives him or her exposure to a life told in fullness and richness, as it offers him or her a dynamic encounter with a human being fully alive.

I try to achieve this kind of writing in a number of ways. In the first place, my emphasis is always on story. That is to say, although I write factual biography—not historical or biographical fiction, which in various ways incorporate fictionalized characters, incidents, or dialogue—I tell as much as possible of my biography through story and anecdote. Narrative is, after all, "a primary act of mind," in Barbara Hardy's celebrated dictum. Narrative is a basic and pervasive way of organizing our experience, of remembering, of thinking, of planning, of dreaming. And storytelling is our chief mode of communication. How eloquently, for example, this simple little anecdote of Jean Little's speaks about her character, about her family relationships, and about an important first impetus to her career in writing: "I remember the day I'd been trying to get Dad's attention while he was reading— offering to sing for him, or dance, or something. He seemed totally without interest; so I went away and created a poem, something I'd never tried before. When I returned, announcing this new *tour de force*, Dad threw down his newspaper: 'A poem!' He snatched it out of my hand. 'Let me see it!' "

Another of my stock-in-trades is what one biographer calls "picture writing." I tell my story through a series of images, snapshots, or pictures. As much as possible, I shun explanation and commentary, and let the story tell itself and allow the reader to draw his or her own conclusions. Needless to say, the images chosen must be truthful, they must be representative of the life of the subject, and they must be telling ones—the seven-year-old Wayne Gretzky out on his makeshift flooded backyard-rink, forever practising with stick and puck; the teenage Karen Kain resisting her parents' blandishments to come back home from ballet school to be a "normal girl"; Farley Mowat's outrageous, larger-than-life escapades in the tundra.

I like, also, to include as much autobiographical material as possible: for example, quotes from conversations and interviews, selections from my subjects' diaries, photo albums and other personal memorabilia. This helps the reader get closer to the subject—get inside the biography, as it were. The excerpts I included in Karen Kain's biography from the journal she kept in grade three, for example, invariably occasion a good deal of interest among readers, as do the working notes taken from Alexander Graham Bell's scientific experiments, and the excerpts from Sharon, Lois and Bram's work schedules.

Because my audience is children, I feel it is important—without falling into the traps of distortion and triviality—to dwell, in a general way, on childhood and, specifically, on beginnings. So I like to show my subjects pursuing what my readers are themselves presently engaged upon—growing and learning. And I like to show my subjects searching as well as finding; struggling and failing as well as achieving; losing as well as winning. Unfailingly, it is these aspects of my biographies that elicit the most comment from my readers as they write to me about identifying with Karen Kain's weight problems in ballet school, or Wayne Gretzky's harassment by jealous peers, parents and coaches, or Terry Fox's struggles with his lack of natural talent in most everything he tried his hand at.

"Biography," as Boswell once pointed out, "occasions a degree of trouble far beyond that of any other species of literary composition." I don't doubt it. And writing biography for children is possibly an even more difficult and complicated business. For one thing, scholarship—let alone artistry—is not bought cheaply. For another, writing —writing of any kind—does not come easily to me. And this kind of book requires a *lot* of writing. As one practitioner of the genre has so aptly put it: "A book of this kind is not so much written as rewritten. It is one thing to have the pattern clear in your own mind and quite another to get it clear in the mind of your reader."

Why, then, do I go to the trouble of writing biography for children? To provide them with role models? To teach them important lessons? To inspire them?

Not for any of these reasons, really. Rather, more simply and prosaically, I do it to give children the experience of close contact with another human being; someone wholly formed who is man or woman fully alive; someone who can help them to look at and understand their *own* lives better. For, as the distinguished biographer for children, Jean Fritz, writes: "In actual experience we are able to see so few lives in the round and to follow them closely from beginning to end. I for one need to possess a certain number of relatively whole lives in the long span of history."

4

Writing for Young Adults
Introduction

There is a large market today for books directed to the adolescent reader. Books can provide insight into the changes young people are going through —their lives, their relationships, their identities. Novels can give them roles for identification, situations for reflection, and opportunities for examining issues. Authors for this audience often tackle complex topics through realistic settings, fantasy, science fiction, historical fiction, and mystery. Children are depending more and more on their peer groups and idolizing entertainment stars, sports figures, and older friends. They are concerned about future careers and looking forward to independence. Some develop a sense of history and their own place in society; others are concerned with justice and the unfair treatment of minority groups. Novels for adolescents allow the reader to engage in a dialogue with the author on a wide range of topics on a deep emotional level. The themes of these novels reflect the development of the adolescents. Often it is difficult for parents to understand the need these young readers have to understand life's problems and they are sometimes unable to accept the portrayal and examination of these issues, even when carefully and artfully developed. Young adult literature has come a long way in the last hundred years. Writers have fewer taboos with which to be concerned, and the "problem novel" has blossomed into a more sophisticated genre, with complex plots, realistic points of view, and subtle themes. There is renewed interest in historical fiction, appreciation of characters outside the present life situations of the readers, and desire for recognition of a developing social conscience.

The authors who are writing in this section are concerned with various genres: historical fiction, science fiction, detective fiction, contemporary life. Since young adult readers usually enjoy protagonists about a year older than themselves, they can grow along with the characters in the series. There is some market now for the limited teen series. But the books that will survive will focus on people with problems rather than on plots that seem to involve people only incidentally.

The Joy of Writing

Janet Lunn

This article is in the form of an interview and reflects the free flow of ideas of such dialogue. Bill Moore is an author and former teacher and has himself contributed an article to this volume.

Bill: Was there one incident or one person in your life that made you become a writer?

Janet: I don't think so. The only person I can even think of who was really encouraging was a wonderful high school teacher named Viola Scott. She had us writing our earliest memories, and she liked mine the best. Really, I was more discouraged than encouraged to write as a child. I painted my way through adolescence. In fact, I didn't publish my first book until 1968 when I was forty.

Bill: Did you send your first novel to a lot of places, or did you "get lucky" the first time?

Janet: I was lucky. I had been doing book reviews for the Readers' Club of Canada which was an offshoot of a publishing company, Peter Martin Associates. I took the book to them and they liked it. They wanted to find a New York publisher and they asked me where to take it. As I had some experience in the field, I said, "Take it to the publisher I love the best—the publisher of *Charlotte's Web,* Harper and Row." They did, and it was accepted.

Bill: As you write your stories, do you have any special person in mind when you think of characters?

Janet: It sometimes starts out that way, but characters have a way of taking on their own characteristics and becoming people other than I had imagined when I started. *Double Spell* was definitely about twins I knew and their mother drew the pictures for the first edition. She is an artist, and her pictures look like her daughters. All the same, I don't think the characters of *Double Spell'*s girls are a bit like the twins I had in mind.

What happened in *The Root Cellar* is that I began writing the character Rose as my daughter Kate. In the end, she developed into another kind of person altogether. But the character of Will became so like my youngest son that an uncanny thing happened. When Nancy Jackson did the frontispiece—the only illustration in the book—she drew my son John! A lot of people thought he had posed for the picture, but he hadn't.

Bill: When you are starting off a story, do you talk it through with anybody? What is your technique?

Janet: Well, writing is an art, of course, and not a science. I think, sometimes, that all I do is muddle through. I get an idea. That is terribly exciting. I write down the idea. I make an outline. The story takes off. I start to write but, before long, I come to a stumbling place. Then I sit down and make very precise outlines. I start to write again. Soon the story goes off in another direction. Sometimes the direction is so different from the outline, I have to decide whether I want to do the new story, or stick to the outline. Eventually, I make yet another outline and start writing again. It's a case of moving back and forth between writing and planning—then finding someone to listen to me read aloud, more so that I can hear my own mistakes than for a critical response.

Bill: Hemingway states that the difference between the amateur and the professional is that the amateur writes and the professional rewrites.

Janet: I have to say in argument with Hemingway that there are some people who do not need to rewrite. I understand that Cynthia Ryland, a fine writer of children's stories, doesn't rewrite a word. For myself I rewrite every word. When I finished *Shadow in Hawthorn Bay,* I looked back at the original version and I couldn't find more than ten sentences the same. The basic story was the same, but I had rewritten so many times that the characters had changed and so had all the words I had used to describe them and their actions. I usually write a book eight or nine times, some chapters many more than that, and some paragraphs and sentences are written hundreds of times.

Bill: When you begin a story do you have a "grabber" in mind—something to grab the audience's attention?

Janet: I believe firmly that a story needs to begin by bringing the reader into it at once. The best example of that, for me, is *Charlotte's Web*. E.B. White starts his book with the sentence "Where are you going with that ax?" He lets us know, in the very first sentence, what the book is about. In writing workshops, I have challenged children to go to the library and pick up any books they really love, to see if that has happened. And it always has. Storytellers all know that if you don't get your reader in the beginning, you don't have a reader.

Bill: Do you have a set routine every day?

Janet: I do. I make myself write every morning. When I am through at noon, sometimes I am happy to leave my desk and do the ironing or scrub the floor. Other times, I can hardly stop for lunch and I have to get right back to the writing. When that happens, it is wonderful, but when it doesn't, I still put in those hours in the morning. If I am writing a novel, I write a chapter a day, twelve to fifteen pages. After lunch I sit down and go over those pages and take out the things that are obviously bad—sometimes I will have tried two or three paragraphs so I take out the ones I don't want. I don't try to rewrite the whole chapter the first afternoon. I think writing has to settle for a while, before it is clear what changes are needed.

Bill: How about descriptive passages? Some readers say they hate descriptive passages. Obviously you don't agree with that because you have some wonderful ones in your books. What do you think about description versus action? What sort of percentage do you aim for?

Janet: I don't. I don't write to an audience. Like a lot of people, I write to the person inside me listening to the story. I don't know until people start reading my books whether they are going to like them. I don't know who my audience is until I get a response. The only recipe I follow is the basic form all stories have. Story is drama, Aristotle's beginning-middle-end drama. With that form in place, the rest grows naturally as a living thing grows, according to its own pattern but true to its own individuality. There is no integrity in a story written to order.

Bill: Where do your plots come from?

Janet: Usually they come from my head but I have a hard time plotting. I am a friend of Monica Hughes' and, as I listen to her talk about her stories, plots come spinning out of her head like a spider's web. Not for me. I always know the beginning; I always know the end. It's the middle that gives me so much difficulty.

Bill: Of all the different formats, which do you prefer?

Janet: I think I prefer novels. In a novel there is room to expand. I always want to say more than a short story allows. I like non-fiction but I am forever wanting to make fiction of it.

Bill: In writing for children, would you say there are any special rules you should follow?

Janet: I think the basic difference between a children's novel and an adult's novel is that both the story and the resolution must be strong in a novel for children. It is not important whether the hero lives or dies. It is important that the conflict around which the story is built is brought to a satisfying conclusion. In one of Rosemary Sutcliff's finest books, for instance, *The Mark of The Horse Lord,* the hero dies. It is a sad and a wonderful book. It could not end in any other way without cheating the reader. In an adult book, the end might be ambiguous and this will not disturb an adult reader. It deeply disturbs children.

Bill: You don't use controlled vocabulary in your novels. You have a wide range. What do you think about that?

Janet: I am devoted to the writings of Rudyard Kipling and I have been reading Kipling's *Just So Stories* to my grandchildren. Michael, aged seven, after listening to the story of Old Man Kangaroo, sings to himself as he goes off to bed, "grinning like a coal scuttle, grinning like a coal scuttle." He doesn't know what a coal scuttle is and he doesn't care but he loves the sound of those words. I do too and I think it's sad when writers don't use all the words that come to mind as they write.

Bill: Do you have reading out loud by people in the back of your mind when your write?

Janet: Always. I think good literature sounds as good as it looks. My husband and I always read to one another. I read to my adult children, they read to me, I read to friends. I have read one of Jane Gardam's books to Jean Little on tape. I enjoyed reading it aloud as I enjoy listening to Gardam being read. I always read out loud what I have written and if it doesn't sound right, I rewrite again.

Bill: You are very good at writing historical novels. How do you go about researching?

Janet: First, I read everything that I can find on the place and the period. *Shadow in Hawthorn Bay* is set partly in the north of Scotland and partly in eastern Ontario where I live. I went twice to Scotland because I have the feeling that I don't know a place if my feet don't know it. So I went there to walk the hills and along the Great Glen, to see and to feel Mary Urquhart's land. I listened to a lot of Scottish music and I talked to people and I read some more.

Bringing Mary Urquhart to eastern Ontario was not that hard. My husband and I had written the history of Prince Edward County, where the rest of the book is set, and I mined my own earlier research.

My next historical novel will be about the United Empire Loyalists, and I am exploring that same Prince Edward County territory again. For *The Root Cellar* I travelled to all the towns, cities and countrysides where Rose and Susan went. I worked in historical societies and in museums, and I talked to people whose grandparents were living during the American Civil War. As I have said to children when they ask me about my research, "When those two girls got on a train in Oswego for New York City, I know there was a train that left at that time because I actually held a timetable in my hand." For me, holding that timetable was a real link with the past. It is in that link that the magic of historical fiction lies.

Bill: Do you have any advice for writers who are just starting out?

Janet: Advice? Write and read and listen to stories. You can attend workshops. You can read books about how to write and, no doubt, they will be helpful, but if you are bent on becoming a writer for children, become a lover of stories—then, start to write.

What's In A Name: Selecting Names for Your Characters

Claire Mackay

Everyone will recognize the title of this article as the anguished query of Shakespeare's Juliet, who, all atremble with erotic angst, hurled it into her dad's backyard *circa* 1594. In the next hot breath she answered herself, something she did quite a lot of, by saying: "That which we call a rose by any other name would smell as sweet."

Reluctant as I am to disagree with the Bard, whose name—"the spear-brandisher"—is both immortal and faintly menacing, in this case I must. What's in a name? More than Juliet—or many of you—might suppose. The name of your character is arguably the most important word in your story. In a name there may reside a wealth of history, myth, motive, and memory, a happy freight of emotional resonance that can add depth and dimension to your fiction. You'd be crazy not to take advantage of it. Besides, if a rose were called a dung-heap I would avoid it at all costs.

I spend a great deal of time, probably more than I should, devising the names of my characters. I think it's part of my job. In his informative and hugely entertaining *Names,* Basil Cottle, one of the world's experts, says: "[The writer] who creates a work of fiction has the wonderful privilege of charting and populating [this] kingdom of the mind, and the responsibility of doing so with names that will enhance the reader's belief and comfort in what he reads." Names have the power, he continues, to "authenticate your narrative." Isn't this what all of us, as writers, are seeking? To make our readers believe, to make them comfortable in the small worlds we create? To authenticate our narratives? How, then, can we best use this power? Let's look at some aspects of naming.

Historical Appropriateness

Personal, or given, names go in and out of style like hemlines. Your choice of names should be determined by the time (and often the place) in which your story is set. In a modern novel you won't find kids called Hephzibah and Marmaduke. Or Gladys and Archie. Or even Cindy-Lou and Kevin. All of these names are out of date. Leslie Dunkling, in his engaging study of popularity patterns in naming, *First Names First,* tells us that in the seventeenth century, for example, Ambrose, Egbert, Horatio and Samson; and Alethia, Fortitude, Philadelphia, and Venus filled the parish registry. In 1980 the top four names in each sex were Paul, Andrew, David, and Jeremy; and Sarah, Nicole, Lisa and Claire (*sic!*). And in the birth column of today's newspaper are signs of another shift: four Jameses and three Emilys. Make sure your names fit the period.

Reader Response

In *Voyage of the Dawn Treader*, C.S. Lewis writes: "There was a boy called Eustace Clarence Scrubb, and he almost deserved it." The image evoked by that name—a kid with flapping shirt-tail, running nose, and snivelling manner—is not one you'd wish upon your heroic protagonist, unless, of course, his name is his problem. Writer Audry McKim claims she could never call a character Alvin, even though its original meaning of "elf-friend" or "noble friend," and its bemedalled World War I bearer, Sergeant Alvin York, should commend it to us. Now, alas! it's irrevocably linked to a boy who consorts with a troop of demented and altogether too talkative chipmunks.

We all have instinctive reactions to names, based on historical usage and on their associations with familiar, famous, or infamous persons. "A name is a kind of face," said Thomas Fuller 300 years ago. What face do you see, what picture do you get, what impression do you receive, from Helen, Charles, Eric, and Phyllis? (For me, it's respectively Troy, ears, Viking, and my aunt.) Whether a character is called Josephine, Josie, or Jo (or William, Willie, or Just Plain Bill) shapes your readers' perceptions and expectations of how that character behaves.

Public figures are especially sensitive to the link between name and image, and freely adopt aliases: Boris Karloff was born the less-than-terrifying Bill Pratt; Frances Gumm became Judy Garland; Archie Belaney chose Grey Owl; Gary Hartpence switched to Gary Hart, not that it helped; and, for reasons I find perplexing, Arnold Dorsey changed his name to Engelbert Humperdinck.

Beware, too, of the inadvertent pun. No character can survive a name like Gloria Mundy, Hugo Fast, or Marietta Lyon. (The unregenerate Peter DeVries must answer for Eileen Dover, Herbie Hind, and Justin Case.) I am quite bemused by the real-life Armand Hammer; by a gentleman in Massachusetts known as Warren Peace; and by a British legal firm whose brass plate reads Argue & Phibbs.

Some names are no longer usable. You can't call a character Attila or Lee Harvey Oswald or Judas (although in my opinion it was a bum rap) and hope readers will view him in a kindly light. Watch out, too, for names that may, to the initiated and aware, hide a pejorative: Samways = semi-wise, a halfwit; Cruickshank = bowlegged; Spenlow = spend-love, a lecher; Thewliss = without virtue (although "thews" are no longer virtues.) Unwittingly, I did this myself: in the first draft of *The Minerva Program* I called Minerva's little brother "Tom." My gentle editor reminded me that Tom is not a socially acceptable name for a black boy.

Esthetics

A name should sound good. The English language is splendidly rhythmic, richly musical, with an easy natural cadence. Use these qualities; make your names sing. Say them aloud, slowly. Then say them again. If they aren't pleasing (and you may not wish them to be, for your own valid reasons), fix them. Sue Ann Alderson's *Bonnie McSmithers* is a stroke of genius. With its linked dactyl and trochee (/-- /-) it is a tiny concerto for piccolo and snare drum. In that archetypal tale about the power of naming, *Rumpelstiltskin*, we hear another kind of music: a deliciously vulgar duet of tuba and cymbal. Perfect.

Unless you're writing a comic (or a comical) book, avoid alliteration. Who can take seriously anyone named Biff Baxter or Candy Kane? (Or, for that matter, Ronnie Reagan.) Tiny Tim makes me smirk, and I couldn't get past the title page of a story (as yet unpublished, surprise, surprise) called *Sammy Skunk meets Wanda Willow*. Point proved?

A name should also look good. Janet Lunn, in *Shadow in Hawthorn Bay*—and listen to that music!—was patently inspired when she chose the name "Mairi" for her protagonist. Although it sounds like and soon becomes "Mary," at first sight—and it's the second word in the book—the *look* of it evokes a sense of strangeness, a whiff of enchantment, which imbues and makes credible the story. With that one name, Lunn goes a long way in "authenticating her narrative." But unless you intend it, as did Lunn, avoid unusual spelling. To spell Caitlin "Katelyn" or Roderick "Rodrik" is to be irksomely obtrusive, diverting your reader's attention and sabotaging his absorption in your story.

A name should be pronounceable, especially for younger tongues. Eschew names like Aglaeia Menhenneott-Ollerearnshaw and Diarmuid O Raghailligh, because each time they appear, your reader will hesitate. At each hesitation, the suspension of disbelief slackens, and finally your book is pitched across the room. And don't choose names similar in spelling, sound, rhythm, or initial letter. I remember—with some difficulty—a story starring three kids named Mandy, Mindy, and Cindy. I lost track of them on page eight, and I didn't care.

Libel

In a society where suing is a preferred leisure-time activity, names can be dangerous to your financial health. Mavis Gallant once wrote a short story in which a major character, a corrupt senior bureaucrat, was named Roger Perron. Her publisher, *The New Yorker,* got edgy and asked her to check the Paris phone book. In it were *three* Roger Perrons, one a senior bureaucrat, degree of corruption unknown. She was transatlantically instructed to find another name. When I finished the historically accurate but controversial *One Proud Summer*, my lawyer advised a similar check. Eight characters bore names of real people in the town where the story takes place. I hit the Search and Replace keys faster than you could say *in flagrante delicto*. The traditional disclaimer on the copyright page won't protect you from litigious maniacs.

Secret Messages

We come now to the final consideration, one which I find the most fun: to devise names that give clues to the character's motivation, role in the story, appearance, or temperament. No longer can we emulate, nor would we wish to, earlier writers like Bunyan or Jonson, whose names were as blatant as billboards: Worldly-Wise, Giant Despair, Overdo, Sir Epicure Mammon. But we can, if we are meticulous and clever, construct names to evoke a response—conscious, subconscious or both —from our readers that will enhance their pleasure and deepen their involvement. And that's the name (ho-ho) of the game.

There is a theory, captured with felicitous brevity in the Latin epigram *Nomen est omen,* that a name foretells the behaviour of its bearer. The notion attracts me—after all, my own name means "clear, shining, brilliant"—and in most of my books, the names, both place and personal, are a kind of predictive code. In *Mini-Bike Hero*, the protagonist is Steve, which, apart from being my third son's middle name, means "crown," and by the end of the book the kid deserves one. The Sunday school camp washed away by a flood is run by the New Ararat Church. In *One Proud Summer*, a story about a strike, the heroine is Lucie (bringer of light) Laplante (young tree, sapling, but with the added echo of lines from an old union song, "Like a tree that's planted by the water / We shall not be moved"). My naming habit reached its apogee in a computer mystery, *The Minerva Program,* where every name has a double or sometimes a triple meaning, beginning with Minerva (goddess of wisdom, something Minerva—and the rest of us—must learn about hi-tech and humanity) Wright (maker, creator) herself. I call a punk rocker, whose hairstyle owes much to Day-Glo and Krazy Glue, Barbara (strange, barbaric) Fairfax (beautiful hair). Mr. Guthrie (gusty, full of wind) is an endlessly garrulous teacher, and the villain, whose identity is not disclosed, of course, until the final pages, can easily be deduced by the amateur onomastician. His surname means "crooked mouth," or liar. And I shamelessly slipped in a private (until now) joke: the owner of "The Gamekeeper's," a video arcade, is named Mr. Mellors, the most notorious gamekeeper in literary history. All of these names are shorthand descriptions, compressed significations, codes transmitting a many-layered message to the reader. Your names can do the same.

I am not, of course, the only writer who uses names to carry messages, both private and public. The small town in Katherine Paterson's *The Great Gilly Hopkins* ("Hopkins" for Paterson's favourite poet, by the way) is called Thompson Park. As a child, Katherine moved to a town in a southern state, where she was miserably unhappy until she met a girl named Barbara Thompson, in whose friendship she found, just as Gilly begins to find in Thompson Park, acceptance and love. In *Look Through My Window*, Jean Little, knowing her protagonist would be a writer, christened her Emily after the three great writing Emilys: Brontë, Dickinson and Carr. Jean also recalled for me what may be some extra secrets in *The Secret Garden*. Can it be only accident that Burnett named the gardener, that paradigm of the natural and the dependable, Weatherstaff? Or the housekeeper, who seeks control over others and keeps Mary confined, Mrs. Medlock? Or that timid Colin's surname is Craven? As they should, these names enrich and deepen the story.

The Judeo–Christian myth, among others, tells us that the first intelligent act by the first human was to name what was in his world, to impress order upon it, in a certain sense to create its meaning. ". . . and whatever the man called every living creature, that was its name. The man gave names to all cattle, and to the birds of the air, and to every beast of the field." Only when naming was done could the business of life begin. Naming, it seems to me, is our primary task, both as human beings and as writers. Our job is to put a name to experience, to catalogue the monstrosities and the mysteries of life, so as to make them signify. By naming our world, we know it, we own it, and we love it more profoundly.

We are namers, all of us. And the names we bestow—apt, harmonious, evocative, layered, infused with "centuried atavistic echoes," and just right—can make our stories and the people in them come alive and stay alive, perhaps forever.

What's in a name?

Everything.

Selected Bibliography

Asimov, Isaac. *Words From the Myths*. Signet Books, New American Library, Toronto, 1969.

Cottle, Basil. *Names*. Thames and Hudson, London, 1983.

—————. *The Penguin Dictionary of Surnames*. 2nd ed. Penguin Books, London, 1978.

Dunkling, Leslie. *First Names First*. General, Don Mills, 1977.

Dunkling, Leslie and Gosling, William. *Dictionary of First Names*. J.M. Dent & Sons, Everyman Reference Books, London, 1984.

Espy, Willard. *O Thou Improper, Thou Uncommon Noun: An Etymology of Words That Once Were Names*. Clarkson N. Potter, New York, 1978.

Evans, Bergen. *Dictionary of Mythology*. Dell (Laurel Edition), New York, 1972.

Freeman, William, compiler. *Dictionary of Fictional Characters*. Rev. ed. The Writer, Inc., Boston, 1974.

Matthews, C.M. *How Surnames Began: The Story of Over 800 Names From Many Lands*. Hamlyn (Beaver Books), London, 1977.

Partridge, Eric. *Origins: A Short Etymological Dictionary of Modern English*. 2nd ed. Macmillan, New York, 1959.

Rule, La Reina and Hammond, William K. *What's in a Name? Surnames of America*. Harcourt Brace Jovanovich (Jove Books), New York, 1973.

Sweet, Henry. *The Student's Dictionary of Anglo-Saxon*. (Clarendon Press, Oxford, 1896. (Repr., 1981).

Train, John. *Positive Wasserman Johnson, Sir Cloudsley Shovel, Buncha Love, Suparporn Poopattana, T. Hee, and Other Remarkable Names of Real People*. Clarkson N. Potter, New York, 1977.

Watkins, Calvert, Ed. *American Heritage Dictionary of Indo-European Roots*. Houghton Mifflin, Boston, 1985.

Withycombe, E.G. *The Oxford Dictionary of English Christian Names*. 3rd ed. Oxford University Press, Oxford, 1977.

The Complete Oxford English Dictionary (and Supplements).

Historical Fiction

Barbara Smucker

As far back as I can remember I wanted to be a writer. I read avidly and I recall always wanting to know something about the authors of the books I especially liked. I wanted to know why they were writers. I was fascinated by biographies of authors and I especially liked one about Charlotte and Emily Brontë. Their love for literature, their imaginative lives on the moors of England, their devotion to writing fiction and their resolve to become authors greatly impressed me.

I was fortunate in both elementary and secondary schools to have English teachers who loved good literature. One of them had our class memorize passages from the writings of Shakespeare, Wordsworth, Keats and Shelley and then recite them together with loud emotion. I assumed at that time that all writers lived in England.

I also assumed that to be a writer one had to read constantly and also write with regularity. I decided that the best way to do the latter was to become a journalist, so I took a course of study in this field and found a job on a small town daily newspaper as a reporter. The experience was invaluable for I had to write daily and my stories had to be accurate and interesting. It was good for my writing morale to see my work in print. I also learned to dig below surfaces to discover unusual characters and buried experiences that sometimes became feature stories with bylines.

My advice to new writers based on these early experiences is simple. One learns to write by writing and one learns to be a better writer by reading the works of good writers.

Those committed to being writers need to explore all kinds of writing and then I think they will eventually settle on a particular genre that best suits their creative expressions. I didn't decide to write historical fiction for children until I had children. I had not been aware of the truly great literary heritage of historical fiction in the English language in children's literature until I began reading the books that my children were reading. The library that I frequented as a child had no shelves of "children's literature."

When I became a children's librarian, I read more of these books and I have become enthusiastically addicted to children's literature—especially to historical fiction. I have continued this addiction to the present day and I think that those adults who fail to read these books have cheated themselves of some of the best literature written today as well as in the past.

I can best express the importance of writing historical fiction for children by quoting two authorities whom I admire in the field of children's literature:

Zena Sutherland, former editor of the *Bulletin of the Center for Children's Books* in the U.S. and author of *Children and Books,* says: "The authors of historical fiction are usually aware that their young audience wants more than warmed-over history. To hold children, these stories must not only be accurate but they must fulfill all the criteria of good fiction. The best stories are so re-created that the people, places and problems of the past seem as real to us as those of today. They tell a good story regardless of the period—so absorbing that the historical background falls into properly secondary place."

Sheila Egoff, author of *The Republic of Childhood* and *Thursday's Child* and retired professor of children's literature at the Library School at the University of British Columbia, says, "Historical fiction is nothing less than the imaginative recreation of the past. The good historical novel involves the reader in a by-gone era, dramatically and emotionally. The reader, and especially the young reader, must be made to identify with the past, to live it in his mind rather than to study it. The historical novelist is primarily writing fiction."

When young people read historical fiction they become participants in the historical event. They take part in the invasions, the escapes, and come face to face with both villains and heroes. History is lived, not just studied.

Another plus for historical fiction is that if written for young readers the story is filled with children as well as adults.

I heard Yolanda King, daughter of Martin Luther King Jr., speak about her father during Black History Week in a southern U.S. college. She said, "A people cannot know where they are going unless they know where they have been."

A young writer questioned me recently about why so many "bad things" happened in my books, such as slavery, war and revolution. I answered that if historical fiction is portrayed accurately, it must deal honestly with the historical events of war, revolution, refugees, prejudices and other injustices. I told her, however, that in researching for my books, I found that along with real characters who were stupid, weak and cruel were also real men and women who opposed evil, who were courageous and brave and responded to the needs of people and were against the cruelties of war, revolution, slavery and prejudice. I include as many of them in my books as I can find. They provide hope.

Research in the writing of historical fiction is exciting and it must be done thoroughly. Often a writer "strikes gold" in a book and finds just the right incident to give his or her story new life! As I research I become immersed in the particular place and period of the history I am writing about. Then I begin to imagine what it would be like to be a boy or girl living as a slave on a cotton plantation in the South in the year 1850. How would I dress? Where would I live? Would I have the courage to try to escape to Canada and freedom knowing that I might be caught and severely punished? I imagine myself in the shoes of my main fictitious character, Julilly, in the book *Underground to Canada*.

In writing my book *Days of Terror* I had to imagine what it would be like to be a young Mennonite boy living in a small village in the southern part of Russia during the war and revolution in the years 1917 to 1920. How would I feel and what would I do when my village was invaded by armies and bandits and destruction was everywhere? What would it be like to travel as a refugee from Russia to the country of Canada where I could not speak a word of English and where customs and dress and living conditions were strange and different? I found letters and diaries written by these people about their experiences. I interviewed older people who remember vividly those historic events. As a writer of fiction I would not just record these events. They had to happen to Peter, my main character, in my book of historical fiction.

Writing fiction and especially historical fiction with its research and need for accuracy of every detail takes time and effort and hard work. I make a pledge to myself when I start such a book that I will stay with it and always complete the story.

An unexpected reward that I have discovered about historical fiction for boys and girls is that readers often find these past events relevant for an understanding of today.

An example of this is a letter I received about *Underground to Canada* from a seventh grade student in Toronto. She wrote: "I have recently read one of your books *Underground to Canada* for an English assignment . . . . I have always wanted to know about my ancestral background and this book helped me a lot with understanding it. I felt very close to the characters but the one I was closest to was Julilly. I found her to be a lot like myself and I understood every one of her problems. I felt the hardships and struggles that all the slaves were going through. I really admired the determination and courage the slaves had."

Writing Science Fiction and Fantasy

Monica Hughes

The novice writer must understand the meanings of these terms, science fiction and fantasy, which have become somewhat debased by both visual and pulp media. Science fiction is an extrapolation into either the near or far future of our universe, as we know it, or a conjecture about the present world in some different situation, which might be as immediate as the possibility of the loss of ozone in today's world, or as far-reaching as a speculation about today's world if the Roman Empire had not crumbled. Regardless of one's choice of subject and venue, the natural laws of the cosmos, as far as we know them, should *not* be broken.

On the other hand, fantasy is not bound by the laws of the universe, but by the laws of the particular world of fantasy that the writer has designed. Within the context of that world, the laws must be obeyed. Magic may be a fact of life, but it is not random in its use or effect. It is probably more difficult to write good fantasy than good science fiction.

Neither science fiction nor fantasy should be used in order to bolster an implausible plot or weak characterization: the only reason for being on one of Jupiter's moons or out in a fantasy world is because that is the *only* place your story will work.

For instance, my first SF novel, *Crisis on Conshelf Ten*, was written because I was intrigued with the idea of people living under the sea on a permanent basis. Obviously the story must be set in the future, but not necessarily far in the future—the technology for living under the sea is already there; the only thing lacking is the will to do it.

On the other hand, *Keeper of the Isis Light* was written to explore my feelings about a very real person, David, "the boy in the glass bubble," whose whole short life was spent in total physical isolation from other human beings, due to his total lack of immunity to disease. Was David lonely? Within what context could I answer this? A place on Earth sufficiently isolated for my protagonist to work out her destiny seemed impossible, but a planet far-removed from Earth would be ideal. The story *must* be set in the far future, since we are a long way from exploration, much less colonization, of the planets beyond our solar system.

Tomorrow City and *Ring-Rise, Ring-Set* were responses to questions about what would happen if a computer in charge of a city ran amok, and what would happen in another ice age. The technology for computer link-ups and total decision-making is very close, while the possibility of another ice age being initiated if Earth were hit by a comet such as Halley is as close as the transit of 1986! These are both science fiction stories, but their reality lies in the very fact that the setting and the people are recognizably today's. One of the first things I learned about fiction writing was the old adage: write what you know. At first I found that very limiting, but if it is turned about it becomes a useful rule of thumb: *know what you write about.* Know it in detail, know everything you can find out about the setting and technical background of the story, far more than you will ever need. Only then extrapolate, which means projecting a likely future.

How do you find out about living under the sea, on the moon or during an ice age? By research. The main library in Edmonton was the source of most of the solid material needed for most of my books. Sometimes a question to an expert at a museum or planetarium would clear up a small problem, but I believe it is a mistake to go to the experts first, without doing all possible research yourself. Their enthusiasm becomes very contagious, they have great ideas of what ought to go into your book and, if you're not careful, it may be hard to write *your* book. Also, the serendipities that can be uncovered during library visits are numberless! I have come across apparently useless bits of information which have become, in the course of the genesis of the story, crucial plot incidents. Don't skip this step and allow yourself to be spoon-fed by your favourite expert: do your own research.

The secret of how to use this mass of material was made clear to me in my second book, *Earthdark*. My editor said, in her acceptance letter: "We found the technical detail fascinating. Now, would you mind taking it all out?" There was far too much. It is enough for you, the writer, to know exactly how the transport system on the moon works. You don't have to explain it all to the reader. Because *you* know, the reader will believe it. That's what it's all about, in science fiction as well as fantasy—disbelief, or rather the suspension of belief by the reader for the course of the story. Research is the strongest tool you have. Common sense and an understanding of what makes people tick are also essential.

Don't waste time on far-out names or valuable words detailing descriptions of clothes and locale, unless these details are important to the story. I *did* spend a couple of pages describing Guardian's exotic gifts to Olwen, but I was doing a lot of other things at the same time. I was setting up the premise that Guardian loved her, that he was very clever and powerful, that she was happy and yet that there was an inexplicable hiatus in her memory, all of which was of crucial importance to the story.

It is much more important to ask yourself: how will young people react in a society in which there is no employment? What might family life be like in a society in which the oldest son or daughter is forced to leave Earth to colonize another world? How do people feel, think, rationalize, worship, relate to family, neighbours, the government, outsiders, in whatever setup is central to your story?

Now that you have researched your background and setting and, hopefully, found living breathing characters (which is beyond the scope of this article), how do you test your plot? Do not allow any flight of your right-brain imagination to get down onto paper before subjecting it to thorough left-brain tests of logic. This may sound boring, but I have found that it is in this process of testing the logic and usefulness of my plot that the story is enriched, and sometimes even completely structured.

For instance, *Sandwriter* began with nothing more than an association of some sandstone sculptures with an idea of deserts. I had no character, no setting, no plot. I began by researching deserts at the library, expecting a story with a strong scientific flavour. Serendipitously I found a book about the Negev Desert and Mount Sinai which discussed the importance of deserts in the Judeo-Christian heritage. At that moment I saw clearly an ancient female shaman and I knew her name was Sandwriter.

When in doubt, draw pictures. I began to doodle with maps of my imaginary planet. A desert world? Done better in *Dune*. What about a world of contrasts? A continent rich in natural resources, another barren and meagre. The story will obviously involve a movement from one to the other. It wouldn't be interesting for a person living in the desert continent to move to the rich one—more tension and conflict in going the other way. But why? Perhaps he/she is forced. How? Various possibilities, concluding with the idea of a "marriage of convenience." My protagonist is obviously a person (a girl, I decide) of importance—royal? But if she had any spunk she would still refuse to go to such a disagreeable place—there must be some other external pressure. At this point I think of the "ringer," the "fifth business" in the story. I make him her tutor. She is in love with him and easily falls for his persuasion.

Which is what? Perhaps there *is* something important on this desert continent after all, something that this person desperately wants. My heroine is to be the willing spy. From the tension between imagination and logic I have the makings of a plot.

Each book is to me a unique event, with a beginning that is clear and an end I can foresee. It is only the middle, the path to that end, that is in doubt until the book is completely written. It is always a surprise to me when I find that the story demands a sequel—that there is something still to be said: which is, to me, the only justification for a sequel.

There are certain traps inherent in writing sequels in science fiction or fantasy that may not exist in mainstream writing. Logic must really be in the ascendancy here. Whatever rules and laws may have been set up in the first book must apply to book number two, however irritating and inconvenient. In *Keeper of the Isis Light* I chose to have a more radiant sun than ours; this made it necessary for Isis's orbit to be greater than Earth's, thus for Isis to have a longer year. The inhabitants will be considerably younger in Isis years than in Earth years. In the second and third books of the trilogy this became a major problem. The inhabitants knew *only* their Isis age; yet it would be very odd to have "ten-year-old" protagonists with the emotions and attitudes of sixteen-year-olds. The only way out, since I could not step outside the time-frame to *explain* the problem to the reader, was to make sure that there were *no* references to the actual ages of the people.

Though I've been speaking primarily of science fiction, the "reality" of setting and characters, and the logic/imagination balance of the plot are as important, or even more so, in fantasy, where most of the research is likely to be in the head of the writer. Maps, charts and descriptions of places and customs are essential, as well as a clear understanding of whatever "fantastic" elements are necessary for the story to work. In both genres, know what you write and your reader will believe your lies!

5
Writing Poetry for Children
Introduction

Writing poetry for children is a challenging and very specialized field. Children require the qualities inherent in all good poetry, and their first experiences with poetry must be satisfying and successful. There are many forms that poems for children can take: narrative, free verse, haiku, shape poetry, jingles, limericks, but all require a knowledge of the craft. Children are capable of understanding sophisticated concepts such as love and death, but they must be in a context that relates in some way to their lives. Humorous verse, parody, nature verse, strong images, in short, anything with an individual approach rather than a moralistic approach can interest a child and draw him or her into a poem. Poetry and song build a child's awareness of rhythm and rhyme, and bring pattern and shape to print. When adults read or sing the lines aloud and share the poems with children, children gain word power for future meaning-making. Some books of poetry are beautifully illustrated, others depend upon the strength of the imagination. Successful poets know both the interests and the nature of children. Children find poetry of special interest because of its emotional appeal, its unusual forms, its brevity and its succinctness.

Some authors write their stories in verse because children respond to the rhythms, the repeated patterns and rhyme schemes of poetry. However, poetry is a difficult craft, especially when it is carrying the plot line. But verse form encourages authors to write in a very compressed and economical style and allows effects that belong only to poetry. Characterization, plot and story must not be sacrificed in order to maintain the rhythm and the rhyme of the story.

In all poetry for children, the author must consider the effect of the writing on the child. Perhaps the best way to develop poetry for children is to read the poems to a group of children, listen to the responses and adapt accordingly.

The poets in this section work in many forms of poetry: free verse, narrative, and humorous rhythmical verse. You must first decide why you want to reach children, and then how you will do it through poetry.

Narrative Poetry

sean o huigin

Narrative poetry is one of humankind's oldest rituals. Every race has a tradition of epic stories in verse. That it is still a powerful and evocative way to hold people's attention became vivid for me a number of years ago in the south of Ireland. One Christmas night in the kitchen of a small cottage an old man sat reciting an ancient Gaelic legend by the fireplace. The room was full of people enthralled by the sound of his voice and the tale that was part of their heritage.

Another time I was on the Aran Islands where there is a tradition of late evening gatherings around a neighbour's hearth. A number of us sat against the walls with food offered and drink flowing as time was forgot. On such occasions each person in the circle takes a turn to sing a song or play a tune or tell a tale. I had never felt confident enough to join in. Able neither to sing nor play I didn't feel I had anything to contribute. After a few rounds of the group and a few drinks and many urgings to participate I finally began to make up a poem about the island and the people I knew on it. Nervous at first I eventually got lost in the rhythm of the words. Shouts of encouragement were given as the poem grew. I managed to weave in the history of the place and my friends who live there. The landscape and the mystery of its past all came together as the poem went on and on. At the end there was great applause and now of course I can't remember a word I spoke.

Being essentially North American it had never occurred to me that such a recital would be appreciated or that I would be capable of it. That night confirmed in my mind the fact that I was a poet and I suppose it set me on the road to writing narrative poems.

Especially when writing for children we should try to convey that sense of total immersion and immediacy. We need to show the wonder of verse that lies in its ability to draw the reader or listener into an intense emotional relationship with the story being told. The conciseness of poetry's language with its concentration of thought and image webbed about by the dynamism of the beat's flow and counterflow should be celebrated.

There's a sheer joy of language that can find full scope in verse. There's a playfulness not possible to the same extent with prose. Poetry should make the reader part of itself. It should make them want to get up and perform.

I try to do that with my longer poems which I regard more as plays. They're meant to be performed and are written to pull people in making their own imaginations and interpretations take over. Poetry remains at its most effective as an oral art.

The first poem I remember writing won a school competition in grade twelve. It was that poem and encouragement from my English teachers that set me off on what would become a career.

I still use the same style with short lines wandering sometimes across the page adding a visual element to the verse. Though the physical shape remains the same the style doesn't. From the beginning it's been a challenge to extend the dimensions of poetry to attract a wider audience.

I've never understood the reluctance teachers often have to use poetry with their students. It's such a natural form of expression and its very shortness is ideal for children. When standard forms are combined with found and concrete and other more adventurous approaches the art becomes animated and exciting. Combinations of these easily capture whilst at the same time releasing the imagination. Poetry has many advantages enabling it to reach those with reading problems who are overwhelmed by the mass that prose confronts them with. The brevity of line and the music of the rhythm provide an accessibility that invites participation.

It's been gratifying to discover that children seldom have problems dealing with my style even on first reading. The short lines reduce the threat of getting confused and the lack of punctuation allows them to dive in and find their own breathlines. Working with them over the years and listening to their reactions has been a great help. One of the great pleasures of the young is their delight in exploration and it has led me to try various methods of getting readers more fully involved.

I've always been fascinated with writing for multiple voices. These poems don't concentrate as much on story as on sound texture and human interaction.

In *Blink, A Strange Book For Children* (Black Moss Press, 1984) I used a device from my early multi-voice poems. The book is essentially a long poem for three voices. Two of the voices can read simultaneously creating a chaos of sound. At certain points the texts come together on the same or similar phrases to create flashes of coherence. The book presents a number of methods for performance and is meant to make the readers part of the experience. Hopefully it also expands their concepts of what a book can be.

I enjoy doing research and love coming across obscure bits of historical information. There's magic about holding in your hands something that's perhaps hundreds of years old and gazing upon the actual handwriting of someone who was living then. What a thrill to find that one little item shouting out from the page that it is the beginning of a book or poem.

Canada in particular has much unsung history. We tend to ignore the events that have built the character of the places we live in. There is a general attitude that no one could possibly be interested in anything that happened in our locale. Such an attitude is infuriating and ridiculous. The only thing that is important is whether something tells you to write about it.

Local history is a tapestry for the writer to explore. We should be creating our own neighbourhood heroes and myths to be handed down for generations leaving some semblance of what our time is like. We should be finding new ways of making poetry relevant by extending it into film or tape or video forms. The poems still have to be written.

There are volumes of ancient legends waiting to be rewritten in ways that relate them to the present. I've done that with an old Irish saga by having it told to me by a giant still left from prehistoric times and living across the bay from my window in a neolithic site. Something like that can have universal appeal with the added benefit of letting locals identify with the past that surrounds them.

Part of the function of poetry is to help us establish an identity in an unstable environment. The universality of human experience should be made more immediate to us in this global age. There are threads which stretch from culture to culture and age to age. They twine and wind together recreating patterns that are part of the fabric of us all. It's a pity we understand so little about each other at a time when everyone is more aware of the world's diversity than ever before.

For writers there's never been so much source material available. The links between parts of the world remote from each other are constantly appearing. The mystery and fascination of these relationships should be used to draw us all closer together.

I suppose that is becoming more and more a motivation for my own writing. In the 1970s I began a long poem which has at this point grown into three books for adults with a fourth in progress. It is not an obviously coherent tale throughout and is more semi- than auto-bio-graphical. It is a reflection of mind rather than life. In it occur references to my past and to settings from the prehistoric past. It involves countries I've lived in and those I'm interested in. Ultimately it is trying to reflect the connections we all have back to our very beginning.

Thinking in terms of such a long project has obviously had an effect on my other writing. Many of my very short and separate pieces have over the years been knit together to produce a series of scripts for multi-media performances. Poetry after all is only part of that thing called art and we should be using all its elements to create a whole.

Having done nothing but write poetry for some thirty odd years it is difficult to think of it as not being integral to everyone's life. Knowing this is a hopelessly narrow view I try to convey to others the freedom and gusto language can impart. Whether I am writing nonsense or expressing intense and powerful emotions there is great satisfaction in the ability to do so.

Poetry does offer joy and release. It is simply a quintessential part of human expression. Whether it comes out as a song or on film or whatever way is unimportant. Poetry is there and it is the stuff all tales are made of. It is not precious and separate. It is vital and potent and everyone should realize that it is theirs.

Poems with Children in Mind

Diane Dawber

On one occasion I characterized the poem as a car. After all, a chief purpose of poetry is to carry us into the poet's world. To do this, poems are a wide variety of makes and models with an impressive array of optional equipment.

It is fun to sort poems into automotive classifications like "classic," "racing," "off-road" and "family." It's amusing to consider form, metre and image as option packages like air conditioning or sport stripes. It's enlightening to map the journeys and destinations of poems—literally and figuratively. While the four-wheel drive usually takes us to the remote camp, how amusing, surprising or shocking if it ends up at the opera or kindergarten. This brings me to poet as automotive engineer.

A great deal of early training in poetry used to be devoted to studying museum pieces. We were expected to recognize the option packages. We were told the itineraries followed and destinations reached by experienced readers using certain poems. It didn't matter that, often, we couldn't get the ignition to turn over or the gearshift to change once in motion. Nobody told us about other models with less mysterious ends, self-starters or automatic transmissions. The lucky among us found these for ourselves. Others gave up or crashed.

That was just the reading part of our poetry training. Poetry writing came mainly as a selection of options from which we were to deduce the whole. Another approach selected a destination as well, usually one with an already-crowded parking lot. Most of us managed a "binder-twine-and-chewing-gum" construction which somehow passed the teacher's cursory safety check. No one really expected to get anywhere in them. The real vehicles we attempted never saw the scrutiny of day, being built in hiding and test-driven by friends. Too bad we never received input from the professional poet-engineers around. Indeed, we did not know that there were any locally. The models we studied were built in some faraway Detroit or Bavaria.

Given all these handicaps, it's a wonder any persisted in building poems much less sharing them with others. It just shows the strength of our impulse to drive.

Downcast but undeterred, I kept on building poems until, one day, a customer came along who thought one looked interesting enough to take out for a test drive. When that was concluded successfully, I was, more or less, in business.

That was fine for a while, except for one thing. Many of the people around me were children. I felt guilty building for adults alone when my young friends knew I could build vehicles but had nothing for them.

Back at the drafting board, I tried the old approach of grabbing a few options and constructing a poem around them. The trouble was that these would not go anywhere. Sure, you could sit in them and blow the whistles and honk the horns but that thrill soon palled. Not good enough.

Then, one day I was building away like crazy. A driving vision grabbed me. The vehicle, when it was finished, was a soap-box racer. It didn't have many options. It looked rough and simple but it could go somewhere, not too fast and not too far, but with a tail wind and a steep slope, you could have quite a satisfactory ride. But a soap-box racer, when I was looking for a classic model, was not satisfactory. Just as I was about to throw it on the dust heap, some children saw it, jumped in for a ride and pronounced it just the thing as they pushed it back up the hill. In fact, it inspired them to try a little poetry engineering themselves. What more could I ask?

TASTE TEST

After rain
the underground worms
come up
from their flooded tunnels
and wriggle on the concrete
squirm on the mud
float pale in the puddles
drowned
I guess.

When the wind
dries everything up
the aboveground worms
burrow
back into flowerbeds
back into lawn grass

back into darkness
except

for the dead ones
that crisp on the sidewalk
curl and crinkle

"Like chips,"
says my little sister
as she tastes.

When this happened, I tried again to do what had worked.

A SUCKER FOR SUMMER

After Dad's home
after Mom's home
after supper
after the dishes
there's swimming at the Little Lake.

Warm sun
warm skin
warm mud
warm water
there's splashing and teasing.

Before sunset
before home
before towels
before climbing out
there's a leaf on my leg

that won't brush away
that clings fat and brown
that isn't a leaf.

It's a leech
a bloodsucker!

Mom sprinkles salt

Dad lights a match
my brother gets sick
the leech falls off
but I won't swim
    at Little Lake
        ever again.

I felt that I should go back over my process to find out what went right. The first thing seemed to be choice of destination. If the poem goes to a moment in childhood, whether my own, my children's or someone else's, it increases the possibility that this will turn out to be suitable for children to read themselves. These destinations pop up when I am reading (especially books for children), talking with others, watching the world go by or just doing what I have to do as mother, wife, friend, teacher or human being. They may be triggered by a sight, sound, smell, taste, touch or story. Whatever triggers it, the poem is a destination that seems important to share, that has feelings attached.

Often, as a child, I wondered at odd moments just what other people were doing at those same moments. This was probably one part curiosity and one part need for affirmation that yes, this was what it was like to be human. It was, and is, at such moments that my breath catches in my throat and I see some part of the human condition so vividly. Occasionally a poem starts with playfulness of language or imagination, but unless it acquires some connection to the human mystery, it is not as important to me. It has the horn and whistles but it doesn't go anywhere. It may be a source of transitory fun but it will not last. I feel destinations are important. I may not be able to predict what hill my reader will choose for the soap-box racer ride but I do know that I have built my poem to make the trip.

Which brings us to the trip. Whether it is the influence of television, the requirement of a type of brain wiring or just the adaptation of a busy person, I tend to base poems on a series of visual shots like a movie with sequences, close-ups, pans, zooms, etc. This visual framework, when translated into words, seems to work for many others as well. If the picture has important feelings attached and if the picture is conveyed accurately, often it is not necessary to refer to the feelings to convey their weight and complexity. The soap-box racer does not need a fleck paint job to convey the thrill of speed. I have gone into this process of visualization in more detail in *Oatmeal Mittens*. I know that it helps me and I know that many others use it successfully too.

If you know the destination of your racer and the kind of trip it is going to make, it only remains to build the machine. Years ago, North-rop Frye, in *The Bush Garden,* was discussing the literature of a country's early years and the necessity for fitting form to content. I think childhood is a lot like a country's early years. There are many journeys and struggles and the unknown. The literature therefore must have much narrative and myth. There is a little sensuality like food and plush animals so there must be a little lyric. As usual, I did not find these fittings of content to form until after I had tried cramming event into lyric and sensuality into narrative and failed in puzzlement. Only later, analysing success and failure, I deduced the reasons. I hope you are more able to learn vicariously than I am. Signposts do help even if I have to get through the quagmire on the way pointed out.

So, build your vehicle for the chosen terrain. Try a narrative for events and struggles and journeys. Try lyrics for sensual experiences. Keep myth in mind for the imaginative and the unknown. Though, who knows, the exception may prove the rule.

We are down to option packages. There are all the traditional ones of metre, form and image. I am concerned, whether I choose a limerick or free verse, with carefully engineered line breaks, appropriate words and the complete ending. If I'm going to have options, I want them to be the best I can make. Poems may go through twenty-five quality checks before I have to stop and go on to the next poem, sadder but wiser. Revision is not only spotting a weakness but knowing when the repair is the best you can do for the vehicle in question.

This brings me to the safety check. If you have chosen a worthy destination, marked a clear route to it, built a suitable vehicle with the necessary gadgets for a comfy ride, you probably have a unique poem. That fact fills the need we have as children or adults to know that we are special and valuable, as well as similar and mutually-dependent. Your poem confirms the uniqueness of your knowledge and, by pre-serving it, shows how special and valuable each person's experiences and thoughts are.

Time to celebrate. You have had the fun of solving this engineering challenge. There is little as exhilarating as solving a tough problem and even making the solution look easy. Others may praise it or condemn it, enjoy it or misuse it, but the enjoyment you had is something no one can remove. It is the only real reason I can think of for writing.

TINKERING

I love beginning with
a clean sheet and
laying down each grease-black
cog and bolt and link
aligning positions
adjusting tensions and
checking for wear.

I love finishing in reverse order and
picking up each clean, oiled
sprocket, nut and washer
spinning the wheel
and hearing only the whirr
of everything in place.

Bubble Gum and Birthdays

Mary Blakeslee

Love of poetry is as natural to a child as the love of ice cream. Little girls learn skipping songs before they learn to spell their own names. Unfortunately, much of the poetry that is presented as great examples of great verse does not fuel their imaginations. They find it heavy, dull or strange, thus stifling the joy of rhyme. Too often the subject matter is either foreign to them or of little interest.

It is my experience that children relate to and therefore fall in love with poems that fit into a few easily defined categories. I should explain that the group I am referring to is the eight to twelve age group; those children who are beyond the nursery rhyme and the nonsense verse consisting of a number of funny words strung together with little meaning. This is the group that can either be turned on to poetry and a lifetime of enjoyment as their interest grows and develops or who can develop a lifetime aversion to anything that smacks of rhyme or metre.

Back to the categories. I have found, when reading to groups of third- to sixth-graders, the first subject that almost always brings smiles of delight and a sudden interest is naughtiness. Children love to read/hear about a child who has done something a little wicked. To give you an example, one of the most popular poems in my own repertoire is about a child who finds her mother's scissors and proceeds to cut things up. The verse which goes:

> I cut a big hole in a dress that I hate
> And another in Aunt Edna's hat.
> I cut all the leaves from the umbrella plant
> And all of the fur off the cat.

brings down the house. They seem to love the idea of another child doing something that they themselves wouldn't dare do but wish they could.

A second sure-fire subject is food. Children are usually very preoccupied with eating, and a poem that describes various types of food (the grosser the better) in a fun way really scores. Of course, there has to be a point to the poem: it can't just list a number of strange foods. An example is a poem I usually include in my readings called "The Sandwich." In it I describe a sandwich that the hero of the poem is making for his father, "So he could watch the football game / With something good to munch." For four stanzas I list the very unusual ingredients that make up the sandwich, then finish with the clincher:

> I didn't watch him eat it
> But he finished every bite,
> And poor old Rufus, that's our dog,
> Threw up the whole darn night!

This brings me to the third subject that appeals greatly to children: the frowned-upon-by-adults bodily functions. Children who, in a poem, "throw up on the cat," "can burp when she pleases," "sort of wet her pants," "spit through his teeth," to name just a few that have brought squeals of delight from slightly shocked audiences, really speak to the third- to sixth-grader.

A fourth area of great interest to the prepubescent child is the story poem. This usually tells the improbable tale of a very strange person (preferably with a very strange name) in a ridiculously disastrous situation. An example from my own work is a poem called "Riding High" which describes in eight six-line verses the plight of Sylvester Sydney Slater, who was afraid of elevators. The poem relates how Sylvester was unexpectedly pushed into a department store elevator which went through the roof of the building and eventually up into the sky. The last verse contains the surprise ending that children love and that is essential to the story poem:

> No one's seen him since that Monday
> But it's possible that one day
> He will quietly descend upon the town.
> There's just one thing that could save him:
> If he'd use the brains God gave him
> And push the little button that says DOWN!

The surprise ending or the twist is a very important ingredient, not only in the story poem but in nearly all types of children's poetry. Children want and expect something to happen in the poem they are reading, and the more unusual or unexpected the ending is the better they like it.

Probably the most satisfying subject matter for children to encounter in a poem relates to circumstances in their own lives. They love to read about someone they can relate to, someone experiencing something that they, too, have experienced. The subject matter can be either funny or relatively serious, but if it pushes their buttons they will usually love it.

The most popular poem I have ever had published fits into this category. It is called "Bubble Gum" and describes in three verses what happens to a child who blows a huge bubble that suddenly pops. The description:

> There's gum up my nose
> And gum on my clothes
> And gum at the back of my neck.
> There's gum everywhere;
> In my ears, in my hair.
> I'm a pink, sticky, sweet total wreck,

strikes a familiar chord in every child who has ever chewed a piece of bubble gum.

The subject matter for this type of poem is endless: wrapping gifts, taking pictures, birthday parties, plugging the toilet and so on. If the subject matter encompasses both a familiar task and a bit of naughtiness, so much the better.

Again it's a matter of the child versus authority. Eight- to twelve-year-olds are just beginning to stretch their wings and think for themselves. Authority, however, is still a big thing in their lives. Parents, teachers, the librarian and the swimming coach, all tell them what to do and what not to do. The poem that presents a child defying authority satisfies the growing need to rebel, but to rebel in a safe way.

Finally, this brings me to the serious poem. Although children seem to prefer poems that make them laugh, the serious poem should not be ignored. However, in this case, it is even more important that the subject matter be something that is very real to them. The only exception is the story poem that tells a tale of adventure or mystery or some other straight theme.

Writing a serious poem is, to my mind, much more difficult than composing nonsense or exaggeration. The delicate balance between moving the child and boring him is very fine. Worse still is the danger of coming up with a poem that is "mush": the worst offence in the eyes of the child. The serious poem has to be real and it has to be sensitive.

Some examples of themes that seem to work, if the writer is careful to be honest, are best friends, family relationships, fears and appearance, to name but a very few.

One of my most successful "serious" poems is called "Hurting" and describes the pain that occurs when a young girl's best friend moves away. The last verse:

> The stars have gone out and the sun's left the sky,
> My happy world's come to an end.
> I'm trying real hard to be brave and not cry,
> But it hurts when you lose your best friend,

always causes the same reaction: dead silence then a quiet murmur of "that's really nice" or "it makes *me* want to cry."

I don't believe children like to read or hear a large proportion of serious poems in books or presentations. However, poems with a serious theme but with the previously mentioned twist at the end are very acceptable and can be used without fear of overdoing it. In fact, this type of poem is often the one the child remembers long after the light poems have been forgotten.

An example of what I am referring to is a poem called "Me and My Friend." As in the previous example the subject matter is the relationship between a child and a friend, but in this case the ending relieves the sadness that occurred in "Hurting."

The first verse sets the scene:

> I've got a very special friend.
> He lives just down the block.
> He laughs at all my corny jokes
> And listens when I talk.

Here we have a child who has found someone who pays attention to him; who treats him as an equal, as opposed to the authority figures in his life. Although the hero of this poem is very young this is not a poem for very young children. However, the older child has no trouble remembering how it was when he or she was very young. In fact, older children still have to cope with people who don't pay attention to them or treat them as equals.

This last verse has the twist that makes the poem fun without taking away any of the serious content.

> We both were born on August first.
> We're like twins, him and me.
> Except next birthday I'll be six
> And he'll be eighty-three.

6

Filling Special Needs

Introduction

The world of children's books is full of genres and themes. Often we neglect special interest groups in thinking of preparing a manuscript. It may be that a special audience is the best one for your writing. In this section we meet authors who discuss several types of writing with their particular point of view. Whether they choose folktales, film scripts or non-fiction, they are still creating materials for children.

Folktales provide strong reading for children at all ages. The context of "long ago . . ." enables the child to explore the universal problems and concerns that have troubled humanity forever, in a safe, non-threatening framework. The deeds of heroes, the schemes of tricksters and the laws of nations can serve as settings for the child's own development. Authors and illustrators are bringing folktales to children, as well as adapting and using the folktale motifs as a basis for their own writing. They are collecting, shaping, retelling, versioning and interpreting stories and story patterns that have been part of the old tradition.

In Canada, there are many political and cultural issues that children require help and clarification with in order to understand. Books highlighting Native issues, both Indian and Inuit, can provide children with an artistic frame, a wider picture, so that they can come to grips with this problem of identity for these Canadians. Writers can share their backgrounds and heritages to give children insight and perception that will affect how they live.

In this section as well, you'll find two different avenues for writers that are perhaps not often considered: school textbooks, and scripting for film and television.

We often forget that writers are required to create what goes into any textbook. Today's textbook publishers are recognizing that children must be given quality material and are in need of good stories, non-fiction articles and poems that represent the child's world and can be handled in the whole class setting.

Filmmakers are being seen as important contributors to the lives of children. Parents and teachers are making use of video and film, and are beginning to select and screen more carefully. There is a growing market for children's programming and some writers may see this as an outlet for their work.

Non-fiction for children is often seen as a lesser variety, when indeed children are able to read information books for their own interest, for personal projects and for school assignments. It is important that we recognize the value of such reading materials and that the books themselves be well done, beautifully written, wonderfully illustrated, and worthwhile as literature. Biography is one such mode requested by children, teachers and librarians that writers today can present to young readers.

In this section, the authors present their ideas on writing to fill special needs that may not be included in an overview of children's books.

New Stories from Old

Eva Martin

The Origins of Folklore

Folktales are part of an oral tradition that is as ancient as the origins of humankind. Long before the invention of printing, folktales were transmitted from generation to generation, from age to age and from country to country orally. There seems to be a need within the human spirit to communicate by means of storytelling, a need which has not yet been quelled by the electronic media of the twentieth century.

Centuries ago, members of a community met as a group to relate their adventures of that day which, as they were handed down through the generations, accumulated detail and became more elaborate, though always retaining the essence of the original story. In Europe and Asia, travelling merchants retold the stories they had learned in childhood and added tales of their latest adventures, which were gradually woven into the fabric of each community they touched.

With the transmission of folktales to many countries, certain themes began to evolve that represented various states of the human condition—the creation story, the sleeping princess, the story of a great flood, the Cinderella story, the trickster tale, and many others. The themes were adapted by the characteristics of the country where they flourished, such as the rhythm of the language and its idiosyncrasies of speech, the political perspective and the physical background.

Are Folktales Relevant Today?

As in ages past, the family is still an important source of story and folktale material, particularly in the multi-ethnic communities that are part of most Canadian cities. Today, church and literacy groups, schools, libraries, radio and television, have all promoted the value and importance of folktales and of storytelling. The means of communicating folktales can be much faster and the audience potential is greater, but the basic components of the folktale are the same. In Toronto there is a school of storytelling; but in many Canadian cities there are small clusters of people who get together to exchange tales.

Characteristics of Folklore

Although the origins of folktales may be different, they always reflect the universal characteristics of human beings. The stories are straight-forward and direct, the characters are strong archetypes, whose motives of good or evil are evident from the beginning of the story. A sense of justice is inherent in folktales—mischief makers usually get their come-uppance. There is little descriptive background, and the characters, whether humble or regal, are delineated by their actions rather than by their appearances. Folktales represent equality as kings and peasants, rogues and saints are all described in the same tone as equal members of society. In a folktale often a journey is undertaken during which a number of tasks must be accomplished before there can be a satisfactory conclusion. The youngest, weakest and most naive member of a family may be pitted against an older, more sophisticated and unfeeling person. "Helping beasts" may help to relieve the hero of his/her burden or the hero may use wit and trickery to cause the fall of his/her opponent. Above all, the magic and wonder of the supernatural is almost always present.

Sources of Folklore Material

Canada is rich in resources for folklore materials. At the turn of the century, Canadian folklorists such as Marius Barbeau were intensely active recording Native, Inuit and French-Canadian folktales. Later, this work was carried on in Eastern Canada by Helen Creighton and in Ontario by Edith Fowke. Early issues of *The Journal of American Folklore* featured the work of Canadian folklorists, revealing the bare bones of Canadian folktales as they were first recorded. The National Museum of Civilization in Ottawa houses thousands of tapes of folktales which are available to interested students and writers to use as resource materials. The scientists and anthropologists who recorded these tales were not particularly literary, and valued the tales mainly for their scientific and social interest.

Primary historical materials can be found in other sources. Historical data featuring personal accounts of adventures in early Canada or letters exchanged between immigrants to Canada and their families may contain stories retold for the amusement of children which may be recreated as folktale material.

One of the most important resources is the contemporary community in which the writer lives. Families of different ethnic backgrounds have much to offer the storyteller. Several generations may live in the same household, and the sharing of stories told by the elders about their youth in their homeland occurs regularly. The oral tradition is very much alive and the tales of one generation stimulate those of another. Stories which have been retold many times may become exaggerated and provide resources for the tall tales of the future.

Creating New Tales from Old

The reteller of folktales has two major considerations: the actual writing of the stories and the sound of the stories when they are read aloud. Because the stories were told before they were written down, it is important to achieve in the writing the sense of an oral tradition, of the original rhythm of language, and of a listening audience. The writer thus first becomes a listener and transforms what is heard into print.

One of the best ways to achieve the real sense of a story is to test it on groups of children. Children will respond to the important elements of the story, and what is unimportant can then be discarded. Therefore the essential truth of the story will not become overburdened with pretentiousness. The use of an audio cassette recorder will enable the writer to tell the story over and over until the final shape begins to appear. The reteller is not bound to the form of the original tale. As the story is told and retold, subtle changes occur arising from the personality of the storyteller and the response of the listening community. The writer who wishes to recreate a folktale should become saturated by reading as much as possible on the subject so that an understanding of the patterns of folktales is gained.

A simple and direct style of writing so that the action of the story is not encumbered by unnecessary description should be attempted. There should be a strong beginning, a middle and an end, and the sequences of action should be carefully worked out. Children are always intensely aware of loose ends that haven't been tied or promises that haven't been kept.

While the most traditional opening line for a folktale is "Once upon a time," perusal of anthologies reveals that there are many possible beginnings—"Long ago," "Once there was and yet there was not," "In the days when the world was full of wonder"—depending on the country of origin. It is necessary to move quickly into the story, to get right to the action, to establish the main characters and their motives.

Character development can be difficult because most folktale characters are anonymous. Very few even have names except "Jack," which traditionally meant "the lad." Many fairy-tale characters are archetypes, such as the sleeping princess, and do not have well-developed personalities. Yet if the story is to have vitality, this must come from the characters who are responsible for the action, and they are usually very definitely good or evil. Most fairy-tale characters are distinguished by single noteworthy traits such as determination, wisdom, cheekiness, cleverness, or laziness, and these traits should be carried consistently throughout the story.

Nearly all fairy-tales contain repetition in accordance with the number of tasks to be done or journeys undertaken. Adults often find such repetition tedious, but for children it increases the suspense of the story as the character makes one more trip to accomplish the final most difficult task. There may be slight variations in the repetitive action but basically it is the same, and should be related as quickly and matter-of-factly as possible.

Don't prettify the stories. Fairy-tales have violent acts in them. Giants beat their wives and eat people, wolves prey on old ladies and little girls, and witches cast evil spells and get burned up as a result. These acts—which are horrid—are a natural representation of the evil in the story which children read at a different level than do adults. Children know that evil exists and the violence in fairy-tales helps them to cope with their own inner fears. While writers should not overemphasize the violence, they should also not allow their own squeamishness to take control of the story. An evil witch may be the pivotal point on which the story hangs. If the story has been told many times to live audiences, the writer will have gained the confidence needed to put it into print, and will be reassured about the effect of the violence on the future readers.

When the heroes and heroines have completed their tasks, the story should end quickly and satisfactorily, not necessarily with the traditional "And they lived happily ever after," but with a short sentence or phrase which will encourage the reader to believe that all is well and will remain so in the future. One of the most exemplary modern retellings of an old folktale is Robin McKinley's *Beauty* in which the story of "Beauty and the Beast" is given modern dress.

When the story is completed and ready for publication, some acknowledgement of the original source material used should be made as a token of respect for the storytellers of the past. Folktale material, which must be subject to constant change if it is to continue on as a living tradition, is not likely to undergo copyright scrutiny unless another storyteller's works are used verbatim.

And, finally, retellers of folktales and writers creating new tales from old should have the ultimate confidence in the material they are using, for it has survived for centuries, and the writer is only the newest cog in the wheel.

Folktales as a Source for Writing

Celia Barker Lottridge

Folktales are the stories children have always had. Before printed books existed, before read-me-a-story at bedtime, before juvenile novels, children heard stories. Some were told especially to them. Some they overheard when adults were telling stories to each other. So powerful were many of these stories that they have come right down through the print revolution to be favourite stories of children who live far from wolf-infested forests and caves where dragons might dwell.

Between the many old favourites and the unfamiliar folktales that are constantly being discovered, it is no wonder that modern writers for children continually go back to the folktale for material and inspiration. The question is, when you go to folk literature as a source for your own writing, exactly what use are you planning to make of this source? The fact that there are many possible answers does not change the importance of asking the question. The writer may find that there are possibilities not seen before.

A second essential question is, what kind of source are you using? Folktales come to us in many forms. There is a body of tales which are well known in English versions. Most of these are European and have been popular for periods ranging from 150 years to time immemorial. Then there are thousands of less familiar stories from European and non-European cultures, which have been collected and published in readily available editions. Other stories can be found in fragmentary or unpolished forms in a multitude of sources including scholarly writing, personal memoirs and so forth. Finally, a writer may have access to an oral source, an actual storyteller. Each of these sources presents a writer with a different challenge.

A familiar story can always be retold. Countless collections of favourite fairy-tales and multitudes of newly illustrated picture-book versions attest to this. But each retelling should have life and at the same time be faithful to the old story. This is not an easy task and a writer undertaking it should love the story and care that its new telling be vivid and honest. Folk tradition allows for evolution and change in stories but change can be distorting and diluting. Going back to early versions can help a writer know more clearly what conflicts and attractions lie at the heart of the story. A comparison of several existing versions may be illuminating, as may a direct translation from the original language.

This kind of writing is actually the retelling of someone else's story and should be acknowledged as such. No modern writer is the author of *Cinderella.* If a well-known collector, for example the Grimms, is the basic source of the story, or if the national origin of the story seems important, this information should be given on the title page. "A Grimms' tale, retold by _____" or 'A Scottish folktale retold by _____." This is information that readers need and it makes a book more useful.

A familiar story can also provide a writer with the foundation and inspiration for an original variation or offshoot. Brock Cole's *The Giant's Toe* provides a new look at the personality and dilemmas of the Giant some years after Jack's adventure with the beanstalk. In *Snow White in New York* Fiona French has shifted all the elements of a much-told story to jazz-age New York City. And Leon Garfield has added characters and plot development to the ancient story of the Tower of Babel to make *King Nimrod's Tower* a rich new experience for readers.

Each of these books depends for much of its resonance on the familiarity of the story referred to. The variation both changes and illuminates the old story.

The possibilities for this kind of writing are endless. What happened before the story? Or after? How was the story experienced by a minor character? What if time or place were changed? How about adding new characters or reversing the roles of existing characters? The two essential elements in this kind of story (other than good writing) are that it rise out of a real understanding of the old story and that it be an interesting and vital story in itself.

One type of variation that is generally useless is the rewrite to improve the old story. Even if the motive is admirable—to eliminate sexism or violence—the results are usually dull and unsuccessful. It is more effective to change some element in the story in such a way as to give readers a fresh insight into some of its underlying assumptions, as Jane Yolen does in *Sleeping Ugly.* The alternative is to look for traditional stories that contain values the writer can work with. There are plenty of strong heroines and people who rely on wit and kindness rather than brute force to be found in folktales.

Pattern is one of the strongest, most obvious elements in folktales and is probably the one most often lifted whole and used in modern stories. This is understandable since young children, in particular, need and respond to pattern in stories. They delight in being part of the telling of the story and in knowing gleefully what will happen next. The problem is that pattern is not enough. *The Old Woman and her Pig* describes a response to ultimate frustration. Who cannot identify with the unfortunate owner of the stubborn pig? *The Three Little Pigs* is about learning to deal with real threats—that's a wolf out there. It is quite legitimate to take these patterns and the patterns of other standard nursery tales, and use them in stories which express something important to the writer and to potential child readers and listeners. But a sing-song familiar pattern with a fill-in-the-blanks story is not enough.

Folk stories that are not generally familiar present the writer with a whole different set of challenges. You must decide whether you want to present the work as an authentic folktale. If you do, then it is important to know something about the tradition the story comes from. Often writers choose to work on a particular kind of folktale because they are familiar with the culture the stories come from. When this is true they may want to put the story in a cultural context. In *Old Peter's Russian Tales*, Arthur Ransome, who lived in Russia and collected stories there, provided a frame story which tells readers about the houses, villages and customs of the Russian people who told the stories.

A writer who is retelling an unfamiliar folktale, perhaps from an unfamiliar culture, must consider how much the appeal of the story is universal and how much depends on some understanding of the cultural context. Any description of custom or setting that is necessary should be worked naturally into the movement of the story. Special language that gives a sense of a specific people can add an authentic flavour to a story. For instance, look at the sound-words Verna Aardema uses in her African stories.

Often the structure of stories from other cultures will be quite different from that typical of European folktales. The writer will have to decide whether it is necessary to shape the story so that the beginning, middle and end are clear, or so that patterns are repeated more emphatically. This striving for balance between the integrity of the story and the necessity of producing a story that will be meaningful to the intended audience is the biggest task of a writer using sources from other cultures. Familiarity with that culture's folk literature and a deep sense of how European folktales work will be the most useful tools the writer can have.

Whether the writer decides to stick closely to the folktale tradition of the culture involved or to transpose the story into a more European form, it is essential to tell readers where the story comes from. This may sound obvious but in the past this information has often been omitted from published folktales. A subtitle such as "A Bantu Story" or, if the story has been considerably altered, "Based on a Bantu Story" will be of great help to the users of the book and also is proper acknowledgement to the people from whom the story came. More information can be added in an end note if it seems appropriate.

Surely every writer must appreciate that any particular written and published version of a story belongs to the person who wrote it. Folklore, by its nature, however, almost always can be found in more than one version. Therefore, it is a sound idea to search for several versions so that your own telling will be as widely based as possible. If you are lucky enough to have an oral source for a story, the only honest thing to do is to name the teller. It can add a great deal of interest to a story if the teller is described. Richard Chase in *Grandfather Tales* and Diane Wolkstein in *The Magic Orange Tree* have given us wonderful descriptions of the storytellers from whom the stories came.

Some of the most interesting sources of folktales present the stories in forms which must be rewritten or expanded if they are to be comprehensible and effectively told. Examples of these are stories recorded verbatim by anthropologists, stories reported in fragmentary form in travel writing and stories summarized in local histories. A writer on the lookout for traditional material will find stories in odd places. Because of the undeveloped nature of these sources, they can free the writer to create a new and imaginative story with tradition at its core.

An academic friend once showed me a fragmentary story of a holy man living in a desert who was befriended by a lion. The source was a medieval Russian collection of semi-religious tales designed to liven up church services from time to time. The story intrigued me, especially one scene in which the lion brings home a stolen donkey by hauling a whole camel caravan over the mountain to the holy man's door. I began to ask questions. Why was this man in the desert? What was his power over this lion? And many more. Out of my questions and my mental landscapes of a desert hermitage with mountains behind it, came the story of *Gerasim and the Lion*. I did not attempt to make it authentic to a place or a culture. It was my story, based on a folk source.

Folktales, whether as fragmentary seeds of stories or as time-polished gems, are powerful and important. They provide a rich source for writers, and, if they are presented well and if the original tellers, be they a whole people, one storyteller or an earlier writer, are acknowledged, they will continue to be one of the richest parts of children's literature and all literature.

Native Peoples

Beatrice Culleton

Bernelda Wheeler, the author of three very successful children's books, told me that in her sessions with elementary classes, she often starts by asking the children what they know of Indians. In their minds, Indians of today still wear feathers and beads, travel by horseback, hunt buffalo with bows and arrows, and live in teepees. In her book, *Defeathering the Indian*, Emma LaRoque mentions encountering similar illusions. As a child, I held another, more dismal image of Indians in my own mind. That image of the drunken, poverty-stricken, irresponsible person remained like a truth with me until I began to write *In Search of April Raintree*.

Emma also notes in her book that powwow dancers and singers in their colourful costumes were often invited into classrooms. She observed that the students were fascinated with the feathers and colour and rhythm, but they paid almost no attention to the explanations of how or why the dances came about, and therefore gained little understanding of the values and thoughts of the Indian people. These observations were made not to discourage the invitations, but to have the teachers encourage their students to focus more attention on understanding Native concepts and beliefs.

Once the misconceptions are out in the open, we can begin to deal with them by thinking, talking, listening and sharing. Bernelda, if she's in the classroom, can explain why Indians today cannot hunt buffalo. I, if I'm writing, can re-evaluate my own lifetime's perceptions, then do my reading and research and come out with a new, more informed outlook. Before I could ever have done justice to the Métis people in *In Search of April Raintree*, I had to examine my innermost thoughts about how I felt about the Métis and Native people. I had to face my misconceptions and stereotypes.

There is a strong need to "de-stereotype" the Indian and to a certain extent, perhaps, define the Métis person. Consequently, what is first required is that more books on Native lifestyles and issues be written, illustrated, and published. And secondly, that they be made somehow available to educators. Native Studies is not a required subject in any grade in schools across the country; but I, of course, think it should be available at least as a supplementary course, or as revised, corrected units in social studies and history courses, in all schools. And while traditional legends and historical fiction should never, ever be forgotten or ignored, it is necessary to take the Indians out of their feathers and beads, put them into modern-day clothing, take them off their horses, put them in cars or on bikes, show them not hunting buffalo with bows and arrows, but paying for delivered pizza with cash—yes, cash—and having them live in houses with porches and windows and doors, instead of flaps of hide.

At Pemmican, when I looked at manuscripts I was often guided by memories of what interested me when I was a child. My first priority was to be entertained. I didn't want to be learning; I didn't want to be "preached at." Reading stimulated my imagination. Good illustrations made me want to draw, helped develop my creativity and helped my imagination with interpreting the text. Working in publishing, I was involved in trying many things: we could mix the textures of the mediums or papers used in the illustrations (we once thought of mixing black and white background photographs with drawn illustrations, something I've never seen yet). And since we had our own typesetter, we were able to try out different fonts and sizes of type. If the writer or illustrator had suggestions, we listened and often we followed their instincts. However, we often chose our own illustrators and matched their work with the text. We also worked with a designer who saw to it that our books were identifiable as "Pemmican books."

One of the most efficient illustrators with whom we worked was Wendy Walsak from Vancouver. She was recommended by Meguido Zola, whose book, *Nobody,* was the first children's book I published. The plot in this book, as well as in his subsequent books, and the plots in those by Peter Eyvindson were all about contemporary family situations. The authors and illustrators were not Native, but I had Wendy depict the people as being Native, not Indian, Inuit or Métis, just Native. What I wanted to stress with these books was that there are similarities between Native people and non-native people. I also gave serious consideration to traditional and historical plots, but I liked working on the contemporary stories the most. These books were for children ranging from preschoolers to fourth-graders.

Bernelda Wheeler wrote her three books, also for children to the grade four level, at a Native Writers Workshop, first sponsored by the Native Education Branch of Manitoba Education. *Where Did You Get Your Moccasins?* is set in an urban school and reflects a multicultural background. The illustrator used two different textures of paper to contrast the urban and northern situations. *I Can't Have Bannock But the Beaver Has a Dam* has a northern setting. Both of these books are told in cumulative sequence. *A Friend Called Chum* has a rural setting and is told in rhythm and rhyme. Her books, having had the input of the Native writer, a language arts consultant, and non-native illustrators, have a strong educational value.

When I first began writing, I came across words I'd never heard before—words like tradition, cultural, heritage, oppression, colonial mentality, forced assimilation and residential schools. Like most people of my generation, I had never had any real schooling on what Indian or Métis people were all about. But these are the kinds of topics that can be used in books for grade five and up. I had intended to write one book, a book to deal with questions I had after a second suicide in my family. What came from writing that book was an in-depth look at the Native people, a more realistic look at who we are. The situations which Native peoples find themselves in today have not made me less proud or more proud, just more intense about who I am.

In 1984, somewhat inspired by having just watched *Watership Down,* an animation about rabbits, I decided that I would write an animal story. Writing *Spirit of the White Bison* was quite a different experience from writing *April Raintree,* mostly because I didn't consciously think about this book beforehand. I had no plot in mind when I sat down to write it.

On the other hand, I have a plot all worked out for the book I'm now working on. I've spent a lot of time recently typing, typing, typing. But I haven't clicked, yet. I do have parts of the novel that I wrote over two years ago and from which I've been doing readings. But getting back into the characters in this book is darned hard work.

As publisher of Pemmican, one of my first decisions was to produce more children's books. I thought I would use Native illustrators and Native writers, as much as possible, and thus our books would be authentic. Then I began to work with consultants from the Native Education Branch of Manitoba Education on our first project, which was *Murdo's Story, A Legend from Northern Manitoba.* I had published a few children's books and had not come across Native illustrators or writers, and I was feeling that I had compromised. But Jim Frey and I talked and we decided that quality and professionalism were more important than hiring illustrators or writers just because they were Native. And one of the first non-native illustrators we used was Terry Gallagher, who won the 1985 Canada Council Award for Illustrations, for the book, *Murdo's Story.* The effort she put into this book included researching animals and birds and trees in order to group them into summer animals and winter animals, and to have appropriate background scenery, etc. I often pictured her coming out of the library with tons of books under one arm and her huge art portfolio under the other. Similar research went into the illustrations for *The Big Tree & The Little Tree,* another legend which originated in British Columbia among the Shuswap people, but which we set in Manitoba. The last project which Jim, Terry and I had begun work on was the Nanabosho legends. Although legends are often thought of as myths, and therefore untrue, they are stories passed down from ancestors. The kind of people represented in the stories, if any, need to be real—their customs, homes, dress, and artifacts, everything—and the text and illustrations should accurately represent the people of the area.

Like Bernelda, I go on reading and speaking engagements to schools, and I have found that the most important thing in talking with younger people is honesty. While this seems obvious, I've met both students and teachers who tell of authors who were uncomfortable and made the students uncomfortable, although their books should have made things easier. I have thought that students would find the Native issues in my own books boring, but they've been, in general, receptive and interested. Of course, in most cases, April and Cheryl have already paved the way for me, so that I've come away from facing unpredictable students, having enjoyed myself.

It is not enough that Native authors and illustrators attend schools to do talks, nor is it enough that books be made available. Teachers often need guides on how to use books and other materials because the fear of stereotyping makes the teaching of Native issues quite unique and different from teaching about most other cultures. One teacher who was using *April Raintree* had her students go out and do projects on the different issues in the book. When students find out things for themselves, firsthand, I think that's more meaningful for them than just reading a story, watching television, hearing something on the radio, or even listening to someone like me talk.

Film Writing

David Dueck

If the parents of the "baby boomers" could be said to have been media naive, "baby boomers" as parents can be considered media sensitive— even hypersensitive. This has meant that the expertise and the numbers of people interested in children's cinema has increased exponentially. Never has children's filmmaking been so competitive. Never have the issues of children's programming been debated so contentiously.

There is a tremendous concern in the 1980s to uplift the quality of children's cinema and there are dozens of schools of thought on how to do so. Groups like "The Children's Television Workshop" have led a revolt against the violence, stereotyping, and condescension which have characterized the mainstream approach in the past. It might be a bit too optimistic to say that the day of such lazy formula production is definitively drawing to a close, but it is undoubtedly true that there have never been better opportunities for the creative individual to produce quality children's programming than the present. The harsh reality is, however, that because of changing demographics, the market sector for children's production is decreasing. In other words, the pressure is on.

When writing a children's film or television show, you cast your-self into a genre rife with contending interest groups and full of warring factions. Obviously those worried about "GI Joe" are going to find themselves at odds with some toy manufacturers. At the same time, those people desiring to curtail gratuitous violence in children's films have to consider that there seems to be natural aggressiveness and frus-tration in children which children's literature and films have tradition-ally addressed and to some degree vented.

The 1980s have been a time for change, not just for children's production but for the industry in general. Some of these changes have been advantageous, especially for the smaller independent producer. For those who are not aware of the economics of film productions some facts might be encouraging: while the sale of ten thousand copies of a children's book in Canada makes it a best seller, even the lowest-rated Canadian television drama on prime time would be viewed by a hundred thousand. A very successful Canadian production might attract a million viewers while the film shown on United States network television could have an audience of 10 million people. The financial rewards from television or movies can be substantial whether or not one is at the top of the ratings. The minimum ACTRA rate for a screenwriter of a theatrical feature is $24 000. The trick, or course, is to sell your script at this level.

The selling of a script or the pitching of an idea is almost as important as the ability to write a good script. In today's market you must know what you are doing. Your script must be properly presented in the correct form. At a professional level there is a right way to lay out a script with internationally recognized conventions. Anything else, to put it bluntly, is unacceptable. When speaking of marketing, there is no such thing as a "children's script." There are only scripts aimed at certain age levels. Modern marketing people are sophisticated. Norway, for example, a country which buys a large percentage of its children's programmes from the international marketplace, has fifty individuals reporting back to the moguls who control their state-run children's television programming. The actual selling of films is increasingly taking place at film festivals and markets. Canada has three or four of these events held annually; the ones in Toronto, Banff and Montreal now have international status.

People interested in writing for children can apply directly to funding agencies such as the Foundation To Underwrite Drama For Pay Television and ongoing government programmes such as the Canada Arts Council. There are local and provincial sources for various kinds of help, including direct financial aid, throughout Canada. Most of this information is available through your central library. Ask if there is a local directory of film and television producers. Usually one contact will lead you to others.

Once you have successfully interested a producer in your script, you are faced with an entirely new set of problems and conditions. Of course you have to make sure that you protect yourself and the integrity of your script, but you would also be wise to try to see things from a producer's perspective. The producer is ultimately responsible for the success of the picture, and he or she must, in the process, deal with money sources which tend to be tenuous and flighty. For this reason the producer will probably ask to have input on all levels. A good producer will not abuse that power and will intervene only where he or she feels it is for the good of the project. Also, you may be asked to work with one or two other writers. Remember, filmmaking is a co-operative enterprise and you should watch your own ego as well as watching out for the ego of others. To further test your tolerance, the director will undoubtedly demand some changes. The director is responsible for the translation of your script into film and that has its own set of criteria and esthetics.

Unfortunately, filmmaking is an uneven business and sometimes a writer might be replaced. That too is part of the game and you must prepare yourself for the possibility. As gruelling as the process of film-making can be, it does offer some wonderful rewards. You will find yourself working collectively and at the frontiers of your abilities. You will be accomplishing things you never thought possible and you will discover that the whole can be greater than the sum of the parts.

The future is bright. New efforts are being made to address the children's market in creative ways. There are now a new Youth Channel and a new Family Channel on the air. The video boom is almost old news. Video cassette marketing has already almost doubled the poten-tial for the production of children's programming. There are schools, church organizations, and special interests "hungry for product."

The problem or the challenge is, as I have said, that the buyers of children's cinema and television productions are "hungry" for not just any "product" but "quality product." This is perhaps the most signi-ficant change of the last ten years. It means that you must learn how to write scripts of high quality. You might begin by looking at the scripts of your favourite children's movie or TV show. With some digging these scripts are often available. There are also books dealing with the basics of screenwriting covering everything from the correct form of a script to the mechanics of plot development. If you live in a large city there are usually courses offered on screenwriting as well.

Cynical people should not be writers for children. Children are naturally curious and impressionable. Unfortunately there are still people willing to manipulate children for selfish or twisted reasons of their own, who somehow find their way into the industry. "The trouble with children," a wise man once said, "is that they tend to be immature." A writer for children should understand that fact yet respect children for who they are. He or she must be sensitive and aware of the magic of childhood. It helps to be childlike but it is wrong to be childish. Chil-dren are a sacred trust and the children's writer must seek to strike a balance between their natural curiosity and those things which children must be protected from. You must learn to write scripts for real children with real fears and real hopes. You must learn to balance the concerns of harried producers with the artistic need to reach out and touch children who are often confused and traumatized by the harsh realities of the modern world. Most of all, you must never underesti-mate a child's imagination.

Writing for Children's Magazines

Sylvia Funston

You're the editor of a successful children's magazine and you've been asked to write a fifteen-hundred-word article on how to write non-fiction for children's magazines. You stare at the blank piece of pink paper in your machine (pink because it cuts down on eye-strain on draft copy), stick the chewed-up pencil stub behind your ear again and wonder how, after years of producing interactive articles for children, you can possibly write a "straight" article for adults. Worst of all, you've got to do it without pictures.

Are you beginning to feel drawn into this scenario? It's difficult to ignore someone when they're talking directly to you, isn't it? Talking directly to your reader is one of the trademarks of juvenile non-fiction. So throw away phrases such as "Let us," or "Now we'll." Apart from sounding condescending, they imply large numbers and simply aren't as friendly as "you."

The correct pronoun to set the tone is an important tool that helps generate reader interest in what you have to say and strengthens your effectiveness as a communicator. How else can you make your articles interesting to children?

1. Base your article on a strong idea, not a topic.

If you were a child, which of these two articles would you rather read: "An Examination of the Dinosaurs between the Cretaceous and the Jurassic Periods," or "What Killed the Dinosaurs?"

The first title describes a topic-related article that, at best, can offer only a general overview of dinosaurs. In a children's periodical with limited space, an overview runs the risk of becoming too simplistic, and is much too broad in focus to hold the average reader's attention for long.

The second title promises an idea-related article with a tight focus. It allows the writer to examine new evidence on a specific topic that interests most children, and also encourages the reader to draw his or her own conclusions, or perhaps better still, ask questions.

2. Make your idea accessible to the reader.

Children select magazine articles to read in much the same way they select TV shows to watch. They flip from page to page, and if nothing grabs their attention they keep flipping. One solution is to provide the reader with several easy access points to your idea:

- *Find your head.* Give your article a snappy title, or "head." Instead of "The Annual Migration of the Common Lobster" try, "What's Long and Blue and has 8000 Feet?"
- *Introduce your idea.* Write a short introduction that presents the idea behind your article and motivates the child to read further. This is sometimes known as a "deck," and is often set off from the body copy in display type.
- *Pass the ketchup.* Highlight particularly interesting ideas with humorous, catchy subheads. For instance, a paragraph on the eating habits of pigs would catch the reader's eye faster if it had a subhead that announced, "Messy Munchers," than if it had no subhead at all.
- *Let the picture speak, then have the last word.* Provide captions for any photographs used in the article. But remember that captions, or "pull-outs," shouldn't merely describe what the reader can see in the picture. Instead, they should provide information beyond the moment of the photograph.
- *Read me, I'm interesting.* Set aside interesting material that's tangential to the main development of your idea, but which adds colour and depth to the reading experience, and put it in a sidebar.

3. Write from the perspective of the child.

An article on energy conservation that explores how much money the nation would save if the steel industry incorporated new energy-saving devices isn't likely to appeal to many children. But an article that shows how much money the nation would save if children decided what they wanted to eat *before* opening the fridge door has instant child-appeal. Once the reader has made the connection between actions and results in his or her own life, it's much easier to show—in a sidebar—how the same dynamics apply to industry because the topic now has relevance to the child.

4. Use analogies instead of numerical statistics.

It's possible to describe the size of an African elephant's ears without mentioning a number. Try substituting a child's out-stretched arms as a unit of measurement. Did you know that a blue whale has a heart the size of a Volkswagen Beetle?

5. Apply fiction-writing techniques to non-fiction.

An article on how light affects you could be written partly as a first-person narrative about a day in the life of an eleven-year-old boy, and partly as descriptive copy that explains the science behind his actions throughout the day. The fictional treatment pulls the reader in and softens the hard science core of the article.

6. Try unusual settings.

A scientific article on the behaviours of rabbits and hares in the wild acquires greater depth when they are examined in contrast to the well-known fictional antics of Peter Rabbit, Thumper or the March Hare. It's amazing how much science can be revealed in literature.

7. Keep your copy lively and conversational in tone.

At the completion of your first draft, pick up your blue pencil, turn all passive verbs into active ones then get rid of third person pronouns in favour of second person pronouns. Next, vary the length and structure of your sentences, cut extra-long sentences in half, weed out all redundancies and try to tighten your copy by at least 20 percent. Then read it out loud to check its tone. Is it conversational? Have you drawn vivid word pictures that help the reader clearly see what you're describing?

8. Surprise your reader.

Find an expert on the topic you're exploring. He or she can probably provide you with a little known fact or surprising twist that you wouldn't find in library research. And make sure your source material is up-to-date, otherwise you might be guilty of perpetuating wrong information.

9. Get to the point quickly.

A magazine is not a book and you can't afford the luxury of a long preamble to set the scene.

10. Think visually.

Children "read" pictures for instant information and juvenile non-fiction almost always has accompanying visuals. While you're formulating your article you should ask yourself whether a photograph or illustration might do the job of communicating part of your idea better than a lot of words. Once you've done your first draft and have talked over any changes with the editor, ask how the words are going to work with the pictures. Then, when you're polishing your copy, remember the presence of those pictures and make them work for you in communicating ideas.

11. Save your big ideas for big articles.

Don't inflate a pet idea into an eight-page feature when it lacks the content to support it. Few magazine editors will assign a major feature to an unknown writer so it's always best to start off by submitting ideas that can be handled in two or four pages. Children's periodicals, especially highly visual ones, often publish their material in double-page spreads.

12. Do your homework.

Research the market before submitting your ideas to editors. A busy publication might receive upward of fifty unsolicited manuscripts and queries a week. Frequently, a large percentage of those are totally unsuitable to the publication's needs. Here are a few fast tips on how to submit material to children's magazines:

- Find children's magazines whose interests match your own. Check out *Writer's Market* and the Educational Press Association of America's (EDPRESS) annual listing of children's periodicals.
- Write to your selected magazines and request editorial guidelines, a sample issue and an index if available. *Writer's Market* tells you the correct procedure to follow.
- Study the sample issue for writing style, content and presentation of articles. Check the index to see if your idea has been covered within the past three years. (Most children's periodicals have a turnover in readership every two to four years.)
- Submit your material according to the instructions in the editorial guidelines.

One final note: many an idea has been rejected because the writer tried to convince the editor about the sparkling qualities of his or her article with a query letter that didn't match the promise of things to come. First impressions do count!

But perhaps more importantly, many writers of juvenile non-fiction overlook one simple, yet vital step in the development of an idea: talking to children. It keeps you up-to-date with trends and children's interests. It gives you honest feedback on your ideas and is an ongoing source of inspiration.

Writing for Textbooks

William H. Moore

Writing for textbooks, which we often call anthologies or readers, calls for all the skills used in writing for any audience anywhere. There are also some additional demands, peculiar to this market.

When you are writing stories, plays, articles or poems for use in texts, it is well to bear in mind the skills which will be taught. The names of the skills may vary from publisher to publisher, but in the main they will include the following:

- Understanding the main idea of the piece.
- Being able to figure out supporting details.
- Understanding character, setting, place, and mood.
- Understanding point of view.
- Understanding the whole concept of cause and effect, sequence, etc.
- Being able to evaluate the truth of non-fiction material, making allowances for bias.
- Being able to appreciate the special use of words in poetry and stories.
- Being able to appreciate the correct use of words in non-fiction.
- Learning how to organize material for presentation to others (research).
- Learning how poets make their poems.

Textbooks are usually for everyone in the class; therefore they must be created with a general, collective response in mind. They provide a place to begin with the large group before sending children on to make individual choices.

Readability Levels

The material must be written at a level at which the reader can cope.

There are more than forty ways of predicting the readability of a piece of writing. Some work on the number of familiar words, the number of unfamiliar words, the length of sentences, the number of sentences, the complications and complexities of sentences. Some schemes work on the numbers of pronouns, the number of syllables in words, etc.

For example, in the Dale Chall formula, a sample passage of one hundred words is chosen from the text. The number of sentences is counted, and the average number of words in each sentence is established. These are compared with a list of some three thousand words found to be within the vocabularies of average students at the different levels.

All this is extremely mechanical. There are massive difficulties with it. For instance, some selections from *The Forsyte Saga*, by Galsworthy, were tested under several of these formulae. The mechanical answer gave an approximate level of grade seven. The story, however, is about financial dealers in late Victorian London, discussing matters far beyond the ken of the average or even brilliant grade seven student.

However, the formulae may be useful, and can establish levels which can help the writer.

While readability tests do have value, the writer is probably wiser to test out materials on children and young people, letting them read it to themselves. Remember, some pieces are meant to be read silently, while others are to be read aloud, perhaps by the teacher. The students' listening vocabulary will usually be far greater than their reading vocabulary.

A good rule of thumb is to try to write slightly below the appropriate readability level, so that the story, poem or play you write may be enjoyable for the reader, and not be so difficult that it deters the reader from learning the various reading skills. If you are writing for a grade four reader, try to aim for a readability slightly lower than grade four. On the other hand, if you are writing a piece which you intend to be read aloud by the teacher, this rule does not apply.

Stories, Poems, Articles, Plays
All editors seem to agree that *action* is what readers want, especially young readers.

Character is extremely important. Young readers want clear-cut characters, people with whom they can identify. Female heroes are greatly in demand.

It is wise to make the story-line relatively simple. Complicated sub-plots are hard to do in short pieces.

There should be a good, clear climax.

As in all fiction, there must be conflict, characters, and, especially in stories for young people, conversation. (Remember how bored Alice was because her sister's book had "no conversations" in it?)

The names you give your characters are important. Remember

that names date quickly. The popular girl's name of today may give rise to laughter tomorrow. It is wise to stay with either the old standards, or with names totally out of the mainstream.

When writing dialogue, the writer must avoid illiterate speech as much as possible, bearing in mind that sub-standard speech may sometimes be necessary. Much can be suggested, though. Remember that in *Treasure Island*, Robert Louis Stevenson managed to suggest hard-swearing pirates, without introducing one single word that could be called "bad language." Some writers may object to this restriction. On the other hand, if the material is to appear in a text, then the more standard the language the reader is exposed to, the better.

Conversation is extremely important and can express action far better than descriptions of that action.

If you are writing a story which you hope will be included in a text, you must never feel that this is an easy task. Some writers seem to think that "knocking off a piece for kids to read" is something they can do without much thought or effort. When you are aiming for the textbook market, it is well to remember that the people reading your original manuscript will be men and women very well-versed in the whole field of reading for young people. Once the manuscript is published in a textbook, the audience of critics grows. These are not just the general reader type of critic. They know what works, and what does not. Their standards are high.

What about vocabulary? This is another minefield, for there are those who espouse the "controlled vocabulary" concept, even going as far as demanding that books be written in Basic English. On the other hand, many readers, and teachers, who will be the ultimate judges, know that young readers learn very early to tackle unknown words in various ways. One way they unlock meanings from words is by getting the meaning from the context. If you need a long word, a difficult word, put it in. At the same time, try to set it in a context from which the reader can guess its meaning fairly easily.

The feel of the word, and the sound of the word are especially important, when we write for children's texts. Quite often your story will be read aloud. Make sure that it flows, and sounds pleasing to the ear.

Many texts contain plays for children. Here is a wonderful field for the writer. No longer are you constricted by the formula for professional playwriting: small cast, one set. (Keep the expense down.) Settings can be unlimited in variety, because the children's imaginations will supply all that is needed.

The story-line should not be too complex. The characters should be clear-cut. Do not forget to write some good lines for the "bad guys." These are often the most fun to do. Bear in mind that in many stories from which plays could be taken, there is a preponderance of male characters. While girls can play boys' parts, there is a great need for plays in which girls do have leading roles.

This brings up the matter of plots. Folktales, fairy stories, short scenes from famous novels, scenes from history, all make excellent plots. If you are worried about not being original, remember Shakespeare borrowed his plots too.

What about poetry for children and young people? There is a constant search for good new poetry to use in textbooks.

Once again, remember not to write down to the reader. Many of the poems used in texts will be read aloud. Most young readers like rhythm, some rhyme, a shape that they can recognize when they listen to it. The subjects can be anything. Some words can have strange connotations for children. How do you find out about these dangerous words? Listen to children. Most young readers are not keen on long poems, with lots of description. Keep it brief, and pithy. Humour helps. There is an enormous dearth of funny poetry. Possibly this is because it is so hard to write.

Many texts contain large amounts of non-fiction material. There is an enormous field for exploration here. Once again, bear in mind the readability level. Do not get so bound up in the material that you forget that it is to be read by a child in grade three, for example. Again, a certain brevity is always to be desired. Children do not like having their science or history or geography presented in a cute fashion. Give it to them simply and clearly.

Above all, whatever you are writing—prose, fiction, non-fiction, poetry or drama: keep it interesting.

Canadian content is always appreciated, but not if it appears contrived or forced.

Over the years various attempts have been made to see what young people like to read. The consensus seems to be that these are the themes they like best: *humour, animals, adventure, patriotism, holidays.* A combination of these themes will always produce a winner (as the Walt Disney writers know).

There are many, many stories with male protagonists. Try to balance things out, and have both male and female heroes. Similarly, it is a good idea to show families which are not the typical two-parent, middle class, suburban type. Your readers will not all come from single-dwelling homes, where father has a briefcase job, and mother excels only in cookie-baking. This does not mean that you *never* write of such settings, but remember that modern society embraces all kinds of family situations. Also, a setting which you know well might seem dull to you; to the reader it might appear most intriguing.

Avoid stereotyped views of all kinds. Canada is full of children from every ethnic background. While their heritage is fascinating, stereotypical situations are best avoided.

Stories, poems and plays with Native people and Inuit as heroes are much to be desired.

Many families in this country are split and separated, and the children do not know their grandparents. On the other hand, grandparents can be fascinating people, who have much in common with children, in that they often lack power, and are often ignored.

People from various religious groups should be part of what you write.

While descriptive passages delight the writer, they are not always acceptable to the younger reader. This does not mean that you never use description. It does suggest that action should outweigh passive description.

Above all, children want fairness to prevail in stories, poems and plays. In the main, honest and fair treatments are most appreciated.

Before you send in material for use in textbooks, it is wise to discover which publishers are currently bringing out new series, and at what levels. Obviously, a company that has just launched a new programme will not be in the market yet. Knowing your market is essential. Most educational publishers tend to pay a straight fee rather than royalties for single contributions.

When writing for texts, all the rules for good writing apply. The readers will be critical, beginning with the editors, continuing with those who are going to teach the material, and above all, and certainly most importantly, with the children and young people who read.

The writer must be good.

7

Publishing Books for Children

Introduction

Once a writer has a book prepared, the next job is to present it to a publisher. This may prove more complicated than it seems, since publishers receive thousands of manuscripts each year and can only select a few for publication. New authors must think as carefully as possible about how they will contact a publisher.

The writers in this section are editors, agents, and publishers, and they present their articles with first-hand advice. To get a publisher to look at your book you must first of all prepare your manuscript so that it is professional looking, adhering to guidelines of the publishing house being contacted. These guidelines are fairly uniform from one publisher to the next, but it may help to request a copy of its writers' guidelines. You may want to talk to a publishing house to see if they represent the type of material you have written. Sometimes an agent will submit your material for you, but agents, like publishers, represent very few authors.

The role of the editor and the publisher may be unclear to you. The articles in this section discuss how an editor works with an author in completing a project, and how a publisher works with an author to build a book.

Getting a book published is not impossible, but it is not easy. The hints in these selections may give you a point at which to begin.

The Role of the Publisher

Valerie Hussey

Imagine this. It's a cold wintry night. A fire is blazing in the living room fireplace, and you're curled up on the sofa with a glass of port and the anticipated pleasure of an evening's reading. Sound pleasant?

Now, add to the picture a pile of envelopes, all shapes and sizes: two hundred of them. For the publisher who accepts unsolicited submissions, that might represent three or four weeks worth of stories that have come in over the transom. A publisher's decision to accept unsolicited manuscripts is an important one, and yet it is likely that only one or two stories in a thousand will be published. That's a great deal of reading—not all of it good—in the hope of "discovering" new talent.

It only takes a couple of hours to read a hundred picture-book manuscripts, which may account for the willingness of publishers of children's books to maintain their open door policy. But a publisher is not in the business of giving free advice, not if she wants to stay in business. Time is too limited, and all those stories do take time, for very little, if any, return.

If the would-be author thought carefully about the process of finding a publisher he or she would realize that it should not be haphazard. After all, the writer has spent time and energy creating a story that he or she believes is worthy of publication. If you asked a chocolate chip cookie enthusiast to describe various brands of cookies, he could probably do so quite adroitly. Ask an unpublished writer to describe the emphasis and character of a particular publisher's list, and most won't be able to.

So what should the writer do? Know what the publishers to whom you are submitting your manuscript publish. There is nothing more frustrating for a publisher of realistic teen novels than to receive a manuscript inspired by *The Borrowers*. Call or write to a publisher to ask for a recent catalogue—but not to talk and describe the plot of your book. All publishers are delighted to send out copies of their catalogue; it is their primary selling tool and they tend to have lots available. Examine each list carefully. By researching your options you may never have to wallpaper your bathroom with rejection letters. You may make fewer submissions, but they will all make more sense. Your local library and bookstore can also tell you about a publisher's list. Don't just look at the titles in the catalogue, look at the books. What is the nature of the list? How would you describe the publisher's approach to your genre? Is it the same as, or similar to, yours? Can you even find the publisher's books? If they're not in bookstores or libraries in your area, that may tell you something even more important about the publisher.

If you can answer these questions easily and objectively, you'll be better able to assess the suitability of your work to a particular list. If you want to go a step further to learn about the publishing industry, read the trade journals or papers. You'll learn a phenomenal amount about a publisher from these sources. Not all the information will be pertinent to you now, but it will give you an indication of each publisher's place, or stature, in the industry.

Remember that once you do begin sending your work out, first impressions count. Illegible, handwritten letters and tattered manuscripts are not warm, inviting introductions. There's a lot of competition out there, and much of it has developed enough polish and savvy to give you a run for your money. If a publisher perceives sloppiness or indifference in your presentation, she is not going to be eager to begin the long working relationship required to bring a book to market. You must think of yourself as a salesperson. While your wares are personal and unique, you still have to sell them. That's why some authors are better served by working with an agent. Agents don't have their own ego on the line, as you do, and so they can sell more easily and effectively.

Here is a quick checklist of things to remember when submitting an unsolicited manuscript:

- Don't call the publisher/editor in advance to describe your story. If you've done your homework, you know that the publisher accepts unsolicited submissions, and you should have a general idea of what the publisher might like.
- Don't send any originals. Copy shops are everywhere. Keep your original copy, with its erasures and white-out and send a clean copy.
- Don't forget to include a return-addressed, stamped envelope. If you spend two dollars sending the manuscript, the return of it won't cost only thirty-seven cents unless it's to say the manuscript has been accepted, and then the publisher might call with the news. You'll believe that the publisher isn't being cheap when you recall that there might be fifteen hundred or two thousand manu-

scripts being returned. Imagine the expense to the publisher. While she's prepared to devote time to reading (or having a junior read) your story, she may put her foot down at the expense of returning unusable stories.

- Don't illustrate, or have a friend illustrate, your story. A professional illustrator knows that the art comes after the text has been accepted, and that the specifications for preparing the art will be determined by production considerations. The novice may not realize this and implore a talented friend to contribute drawings to enhance the story. The story comes first. Also, when you present a package of story and art, the publisher must like two elements instead of just one. It's possible that your story will be returned because the art is unprofessional or not to the publisher's liking. Unless you consider yourself to be equally adept at illustration and writing don't consider a package. Stick with what you do best, and maximize your chances of having something accepted.

Don't be offended if your manuscript comes back with a form letter. The publisher doesn't have time to respond to each submission in a considered manner. It's not an indication of indifference, simply too few hours in a day.

One of the difficult decisions a publisher makes when reviewing manuscripts is when to make comments. There are times when a story stands out; not enough to warrant publication, but enough to justify encouragement. How much can, and should, the publisher say without giving the writer false hope? An eager writer will frequently take any praise as an indication of firm interest. Usually this is not the case. Look critically at any comments that are made. If the publisher is seriously interested in the work, she will say so—directly. General comments and encouragement are fine, and may prove to be quite helpful, but don't assume it is the first step to a contract.

It is important to remember that each publisher expresses an opinion when she responds to your work. It may be a professional opinion, but still it is just one opinion. Everyone has heard stories of the book that was rejected again and again only to go on to become an outstanding, award winning, best seller.

You can assume that the publisher's opinion is based on a solid foundation of experience, and that the process is not as fickle as liking something one day and not liking it the next. While style varies from one publishing house to the next, and style is partly what you are evaluating when looking for the perfect publisher for your work, most publishers are likely to apply similar criteria to the work.

The kinds of questions a publisher is likely to ask when reading your story are:

- What is the point of the story?
- Who is it intended for?
- Is the situation well observed?
- Does it extend the reader's perceptions or understanding in any significant way?
- Are the situations and resolutions innovative, original or funny?

This list is not original, but it is practical. With every publication the publisher asks why a particular book deserves to be published—what there is about it that will justify its sharing space with those which have preceded it and served as models.

While you can't expect or ask much of a publisher who has turned down your story, it is important to understand what you can expect of the publisher who has accepted your work. The first thing to remember is that publishing is a business; if a publisher doesn't publish, she'll go out of business. She is not an adversary who is going to take away your story and try to ruin it with terrible illustrations and poor marketing. She wants to publish it well so that both you and she succeed. This is your shared goal.

Your publisher will have opinions about how and when the work should be published. These decisions are the publisher's, but you have a right to know how and why they were made. If you remember that you are working together, then you won't feel intimidated by the process. Your opinions and ideas may not reflect the years of experience that the publisher has, but their originality may make them worthy of consideration. Don't be afraid to share your thoughts, and don't assume they will be automatically be accepted or rejected. Like most things, publishing is a process that takes time.

Signing a book contract should not feel like you are signing your life away, but it should mean that you are prepared to trust the publisher and believe that she will act in your best interest. If you don't feel sure of that from the start, find another publisher, fast.

Once the contract is signed, the publisher assumes responsibility for all the production, marketing and promotion of your book. If you are asked to make a financial contribution at any point in the process, you haven't done your homework: you're dealing with a vanity press, which means you pay the costs. There are legitimate uses of a vanity, or self-publication, system, but they are not to be confused with a traditional publishing house.

Production can be a huge grey area for most beginning authors.

The "whys" of producing a book in a particular format are numerous. Cost is a primary factor, but not the only one. Again, ask your publisher why something is the way it is, but be prepared to accept her answers as a reflection of the total publishing programme, and not just a reflection of your book. There are many decisions made that affect your book that are actually tied to other books.

Marketing and promotion are two different functions that go hand in hand. A publisher will have an overall marketing strategy into which your book fits. The promotion of a list and the promotion of individual titles is part of the marketing plan. Marketing is basically selling. Promotion and publicity is positioning the book so that the sales materialize. Promotion of children's books is different than that for adult books. There tends to be much less of it, and a good deal of the promotion is directed to primary buyers such as librarians, wholesalers or teachers. That means you won't see a full page ad for your first picture-book in *Maclean's*.

Once your book is published, your work is not over. It's true that not all authors are equally promotable, but your efforts and contribution to promotion are important to the success of the book. You should let your publisher know all the details of your life that can enhance the sale of the book. It may not be relevant that you were a Girl Guide when you were ten years old, but it may be very valuable to know that you are the district leader for the Girl Guides of Southern Manitoba. Bookstores are not the only place books are sold. Your publisher will constantly be finding new markets for the entire list, and your book will be part of that.

There is not a great deal you can do in terms of marketing your own book; that, in fact, is why you've gone to a publisher. You will have friends and relatives who will go from store to store looking for your book. Some place special orders whenever they can't locate it, others simply ask and act surprised if the bookstore doesn't have it. And you will become adept at rearranging shelves without being noticed so that your book appears face out while all others are spine out on the bookshelf.

If withstanding rejection letters posed serious health problems for you early on, you have another challenge to your physical and mental well-being once your book is published. It will seem to you and to everyone who loves you that your book isn't anywhere to be found. This can be very discouraging, and it's the one call to which publishers don't respond well. It takes time to become established. Bookstores stock thousands of books, most in quantities of one or two copies. If a store took two copies of your book, they may have actually sold them, which would account for the books not being there. Or, the bookstore may be waiting to see how the book is received by reviewers. Or, even, if you are going to write another book and therefore establish yourself as a serious "writer" of books for children.

Keep your spirits high by remembering that most success doesn't come overnight. It takes years to feel a sense of facility and accomplishment in any trade or profession. Tell those well-meaning friends that your first book is doing well; that it's not in the bookstores because the store has sold it and it's not in the library because it's been taken out. Then go home and get to work on your second, third and fourth books, and you'll be amazed to see how the stature of your work increases the more you produce and the better you become. And isn't that the way it should be?

The Editor

Stanley Skinner

During the thirty years that I have been a professional book editor, I've played a variety of roles for my authors. I've been a critical reader of their manuscripts, I've been their guide through the complexities of publishing, I've been a corrector of their mistakes, I've been a creator who helped them shape their books, and I've been an interfering busybody.

So what do *you* expect from your editor? In the following pages, I will discuss what an editor does, and that should help you relate to this person when you first meet. If each of you understands what the other contributes to the finished book, it will help to create harmony between you.

I am only going to discuss *commercial* publishing, that means I will refer to those publishers who are willing to invest in an author's talent and pay her a portion of the sales revenue. (The opposite of that situation is "vanity" or "subsidy" publishing, where the author pays to get her book into print.)

At the beginning of your relationship, you offer the publisher your manuscript; if he accepts it, he will pay for all of the costs involved in getting it to its potential buyers. The publisher bets on your talent attracting enough buyers to make it worth spending time and money on your behalf.

How do author and publisher meet? For the author, the most obvious way is to find those publishing houses that have published books similar to that which you are planning. Another way is to approach a literary agency; you can find their names in the *Yellow Pages*. Or you can write to a number of publishers; again, the *Yellow Pages* is a handy source for addresses.

Once you have found the name of a suitable publisher, the simplest and most professional way to proceed is to send a *query letter*. The query letter is actually three things: a short covering letter, a table of contents, and a sample piece of text and/or art. The advantages of using a query letter are that, first, you get a publisher's reaction before you spend too much time on the project; second, you are likely to get your submission read quickly; and, finally, you save the hassle of packing and mailing a bulky manuscript.

Start out with a positive attitude: the publisher *does* want to hear from you. Forget all those horror stories about publishers losing manuscripts, editors not acknowledging receipt of manuscripts, and projects being bounced around for ages then rejected. Some of those stories are no doubt true, but what is more important than those negatives is the fact that new titles are published every day, which means that publishers do accept manuscripts and that books are published. And that, in turn, means that authors are successful.

To which you may respond, but what are *my* chances? Rather than giving a glib answer, let my answer gradually emerge from this discussion.

Writing and publishing are subjective activities. You have your tastes, and so does the editor. As do the reviewer and the book buyer. Those sets of tastes obviously don't clash, because books get published and bought. But the matter of subjectivity is critical when your manuscript reaches the editor's desk. The editor's task is to evaluate it, to answer the questions: is the manuscript good? is it suitable for our house? is there room for it in our publishing schedule? will the public buy it?

How does the editor answer those questions? Fortunately for both sides, the editor's tastes are acquired in much the same way as the author's: from upbringing, education, training and professional experience. However, you must bear in mind that the editor's first decisions are made with an eye to keeping the publishing house in business; his responsibilities are to acquire publishable manuscripts and to ready them for publication. The editor is thus the key to keeping the house supplied with material that will not only produce revenue but will also maintain its credibility and reputation.

In these early stages, the editor is responding subjectively to your work; and you, of course, were being subjective as you were creating. But aside from creativity, an important aspect of subjectivity in the commercial world is risk. Fortunately, the editor (and publisher) is not risking the same thing as the author, which is why it is critical that each knows and appreciates the other's situation.

Once the publisher agrees to accept your manuscript, the relationship takes on a completely businesslike tone: a contract has to be drawn up, agreed to and signed. A point worth remembering is that a contract is only the formalizing of an agreement: if you don't like something in the contract, either take it out or don't sign the document.

Publishing houses differ regarding which of their staff conducts the negotiations with authors; in some houses, it is an executive, whereas in others individual editors negotiate with "their" authors. No matter which person you deal with, you should ensure that what is offered you in the contract and what obligations you undertake are fully explained.

Not many lawyers deal with the world of creativity, copyright, subsidiary rights and book marketing; so that it may sometimes be difficult to get a truly helpful legal opinion of the contract. However, if you publish with one of the established Canadian houses, you will be treated fairly. You can get professional advice from a couple of sources; the Writers Union sells an explanatory booklet on negotiating and also sells a model contract; the Canadian Authors Association's publication *Canadian Writer's Guide* has sections on contracts and other business matters.

Let us assume that a publishing house is interested in your project, that you have finished the manuscript, and have sent it to them. (By the way, I'm using the word manuscript to cover text and artwork.)

The editor receives and reads your manuscript. When an editor reads, it is as a professional: he or she is performing a technical task. This reading is the opposite of what might happen if you were to ask friends or relatives to read your manuscript. They would probably say that it was good—they wouldn't want to hurt your feelings by pointing out errors or weak spots. But such readers don't usually have the training or the experience to judge a manuscript, which is why it is the editor who gives the work its first, critical read.

At this stage, the editor's priority is to ensure that the manuscript is complete, that all its parts are present and fit together; the work must be cohesive. The editor is starting *substantive editing,* which is a rigorous examination of the total manuscript. In this editing, he is concerned with such major aspects of the manuscript as structure, plot, characters, dialogue and description.

During substantive editing, the editor might not actually alter the manuscript. Rather, while reading, he will write the notes on his reactions to the manuscript, along with ideas and suggestions. Once written up as a formal letter or report, these notes will serve either as the basis for discussion at a meeting between the author and editor, or they might be sent to the author along with an explanatory letter.

For a first-time author, so many things can go wrong at this early stage, simply from ignorance or misinterpretation, that it is almost imperative that she and the editor meet to talk about the manuscript. In such a discussion, the editor can go beyond details of editing to explain what is going to happen in the ensuing publishing process. A willingness on the part of the author to learn the process and to co-operate in it, and an equal willingness on the part of the editor to appreciate the author's concerns, will speed the process and help prevent clashes.

The author need not accept any of the editor's ideas or suggestions. However, given that the editor is part of a professional team—the one that she chose!—it is surely folly for the author to ignore his views. At the minimum, she should acknowledge the editor's ideas and suggestions in order to establish what each is intended to achieve and what is likely to occur if any is ignored. It's worth remembering that although the publishing house needs to keep its authors, it is the author's name that appears on the book.

Once these early discussions have been successfully completed, the editor can really start to edit. Always, the editor is looking ahead: visualizing the book in the marketplace. All work on the manuscript will, therefore, be aimed at making it attractive, understandable, and appealing to the potential buyer. The good editor will not attempt to supplant the author; here, he will be using his experience to help the author shape the manuscript.

As he works, the editor will be considering technical matters that range from style and paragraph structure to grammar and usage. Style is a tricky word because it might be referring to the way in which an author chooses and arranges words in a story or it might be referring to the way in which a publishing house deals with the niceties of grammar, usage and spelling.

The first of these styles is a delicate area for you and the editor to discuss, simply because it is "you." The second kind of style is easier to discuss because it is almost always a concern of the publishing house alone. This latter "style" is usually based on the publishing house's decision to use one of the many style guides that have been published. Each publishing house decides for itself which of the guides suits its purposes, then everyone in house follows its dictates. The house has not made a decision about right or wrong, but has solved the problem of constantly having to decide amongst the many variations that exist in our language.

By now, the editor will have put pen or pencil to your manuscript, and will be deleting, changing, adding and suggesting. If you, as author, are aware that the editor is taking those kinds of liberties with your manuscript, you are uptight—and rightly so. But your anxieties should be eased by the knowledge that your contract assures you the right to see any major changes that the editor has made.

To simplify that process, some editors write the changes on

gummed strips and attach them to the manuscript; other editors write the notes about major changes and include them as a report when the edited manuscript is sent back to the author; other editors make notes on the manuscript itself. Many of the smaller details, such as spelling and factual details, may be left to a *line* or *copy* editor (possibly a junior editor) to check.

At some point, the editing process has to be deemed to be finished so that the manuscript can be sent through the production process. I referred earlier to the manuscript fitting into the house's publishing schedule; that can mean both the publisher's marketing plan to put certain titles onto the market at specific times, and it can mean the timetable by which the publisher moves titles through the various mechanical processes involved in transforming manuscripts into books.

Depending on your contract, you may or may not be involved with the production process; again, my advice is that having chosen a publisher, trust him to do as well for you as he has for other authors (as demonstrated by his published books). If you are curious and want to be educated as to what is happening to your baby, talk to the editor; he will appreciate your interest and involvement.

The first piece of evidence that you will have of transformation of your manuscript will be the arrival of the *galleys*. (A galley is a measure of a length of type; it is usually 22 inches long.) The galley demonstrates that the words on your manuscript have now been *typeset*; the purpose of the galley is to allow you to proofread that typesetting. Proofreading can be the cause of much dissension between author and publisher; but this can be avoided if you understand the purpose of this step. As the author, you have an obligation to read the galleys in order to ensure that what was on the final, edited manuscript has been typeset.

The problems that arise at this stage stem from a psychological factor: you are looking at an entirely new presentation of your words. The typesetting on the galley looks so formal that you are likely to read it as though someone else wrote it. You must avoid the great sin of proofreading: rewriting. (Whether you participate in other steps in the production process will depend on your contract; most publishers insist on reserving the right to determine the manner of production.)

The only other obligation remaining to most authors concerns promotion (sometimes called publicity or advertising); the purpose of this activity is to make the reading public aware of you and your book. This can be another tricky area between author and publisher. Problems can arise here because most contracts state that the publisher will spend time and money on the book's promotion; however, since the promotion budget is based on estimated sales revenue, the author's view of the budget may be radically different from that of the publisher. Remember that it *is* to everyone's advantage to have good sales, so the promotion budget is probably appropriate.

One last, all-too-human, point. There are occasions when an author feels that she is not being treated properly by her editor. The obvious action is to go above the editor's head to the boss—"you've got to lean on the editor!" If you choose to do this, bear in mind that those two work together, so the boss may already know about the situation. However, if you have a solid case to make, the boss will try hard to correct it in your favour. As I said above, the strength of a publishing house lies in its authors.

The Role of the Agent

Joanne Kellock

'Twas brillig, and the slithy toves
    Did gyre and gimble in the wabe:
All mimsy were the borogoves,
    And the mome raths outgrabe.

"Beware the Jabberwock, my son!
    The jaws that bite, the claws that catch!
Beware the Jubjub bird, and shun
    The frumious Bandersnatch!"

This first stanza explains nicely the first three to five years in the life of the independent literary agent. The second the blight of most writers. We stumble about thinking good manuscripts extraordinary, bad manuscripts good, and this year's bad idea good just because it was good last year. Terrified of that first trip to New York to meet with the world's really big editors. Will any actually agree to meet with a new agent from Western Canada? Will they have ever heard of Edmonton? Will they have ever heard of Montana? No. Much patience required, but keep dialling and we finally do find ourselves with eighteen appointments with the really big New York editors. Later, we blush to recall the lousy properties presented that first trip. Blush to remember not being certain of actually doing it right. Right, like the big New York agents of whom we had all read about in *Publishers Weekly*. The same terror striking the same year in London, to meet New York equivalents, only to discover not only are they really big editors, but they are also Lord so-and-so, Lady so-and-so, Sir or Dame, and competent too.

    Aghast to read five years later, a profile of an American lady who set up an agency in Paris and who said, "The first eight years were very tough but now things are getting better." Ten years to break-even point. Wonderful! A small fact experienced agents keep close to their hearts. Jabberwocks all. Consoling to think they too found the first eight years very tough.

"The time has come," the Walrus said
"To talk of many things . . ."

- What a literary agent is.
- When you need a literary agent.
- Where you find a literary agent.
- Why you need a literary agent.
- Who the best agent will be for you.

What a Literary Agent Is

Part Walrus, part Carpenter, part Mad Hatter, a very determined person who works for her clients. Her writers. Many-faceted, and often a combination of the Walrus at his best—hard-nosed, tough negotiator—and the Carpenter at his best—careful builder of the careers of her clients.

An easy part of the job, and a very pleasant part it is indeed, is meeting with editors. Agents can assume editors are bright and love books. Individually, and not unlike most of us, they like certain kinds of books better than others, and they know their areas of interest very well. The agent had better have at least a nodding acquaintance with these areas of interest, and she had better know very well the proposals and manuscripts she wishes to sell to each individual editor.

A hard part of the job is that first meeting with a prospective client after reading the client's submission. The first question is: does the agent feel comfortable with this person? Is this person professional? That is, will he take kindly to suggestions for corrections, requests for possible changes to character and plot? If not, then the particular agent may decide, no matter how brilliant the manuscript, not to act for this particular writer.

Another easy part of the job is the joy felt upon the discovery of a brand new talent. That first, extraordinarily professional, written attempt which will interest lots of editors, and will be quickly snapped up by a major house for a handsome advance. Yes, all agents multiple submit. Another hard part of the job is the negotiation of contracts between the author and publisher. Vetting each contract represents two to three solid hours of work. An author, *sans* agent, on the other hand whose first manuscript—oh, joy of all joys—has been accepted for publication, usually signs on the dotted line. Amazing, but did you know that few authors bother to read the contract? Fewer know they have just signed away all rights to film, television, video, drama, anthology, et cetera, for as long as the book shall remain in print. Say you have written a best-seller, then those rights are gone throughout the world in perpetuity. Because chances are the book will be in print somewhere in the world until the year dot. Publishers are in business to make money. So, their contracts include all rights now and forever. Bandersnatchs all. You will receive your cake, but little in the way of oysters and "Beautiful Soup, So rich and green . . .''

"I'll be the Judge, I'll be the Jury," said the agent who is more Carpenter than Walrus, because it is important to her that you get it just right. Sometimes you need only to be set upon the right track. To be convinced it may be too early in your career to write the great Canadian work for children, so why not try writing for the market? Writing for those children who actually read books. In other words, go commercial. Publishers will love you. So will agents.

Agents do make mistakes. The biggest mistake is thinking, yes, here indeed is a glimmer of talent, where there is really none at all. Mistaking a new and unique idea for writing talent. The agent offers editorial advice; makes appropriate suggestions in terms of structure, style, character development and so on and on, and back comes the manuscript within two weeks with a handful of commas scattered about. She writes many cheerful, pleasant letters, stupidly offering more editorial advice. Advice which reads remarkably like that offered before. It really is a good idea. However, many neophytes never give up. Some have been known to resubmit nine and ten times with no more effort expended than the addition of yet more commas and perhaps the odd colon. The agent despairs. She suggests the writer try another agent. She suggests he submit to publishers cold turkey. Publishing directories not only list publishers, but dozens of agents. Well, don't they? This kind of scenario sometimes extends over years. No one enjoys being really unpleasant. Jabberwocks? Not us.

Many months out of the year you will find your agent is not at her office. No, she is out beating the streets of Toronto, New York, London, Frankfurt, Bologna and wherever the American and Canadian Booksellers Convention happens to be that particular year. She has your newest manuscript firmly in hand, and is trying very hard to sell it. She doesn't just saunter off to these exotic and glamorous places without first carefully planning an itinerary: appointments with editors, but only those editors who will be interested in material ready for submission this trip. She makes certain to leave time to visit with any clients she might have in any of these exotic and glamorous places. Arrived back at the office she has, first, to take care of much follow-up correspondence, and then to deal with telephone messages and the waiting post office bag. So, please understand that the distress line is not always open for those long telephone conversations about "the work," "personal problems" and "writer's block."

When You Need a Literary Agent

> . . . nor did Alice think it so *very* much out of the way
> to hear the Rabbit say to itself "Oh dear! Oh dear! I
> shall be too late!"

More often writers approach agents too early. We are not interested in reading first drafts. We are interested if your manuscript is as perfect as you can possibly make it. We are not interested in how much your spouse, girl-friend/boy-friend, mother, children or best friend like it. We are interested in comments from other writers and/or publishing professionals. You honestly feel you have completed your apprenticeship. You have honed your craft. You know all there is to know about grammar, spelling and punctuation. You have read every book available in your local library representative of your chosen kind of children's work. Your masterpiece is finished. It is brilliant. You just know editors will love it and publishers will fight to acquire it, so why on earth should you pay an agent 15 percent? So, much in the manner of the White Rabbit, for fear of being too late, you have sent off copies to New York and Toronto. Often to publishers who rarely, if ever, publish a children's book. Often to editors whose areas of interest are sports or World War II. You have received many pink slips which say things like: "Our publishing programme is filled to 1995." "Your material does not fit our current list." Or, and the most crushing insult, no response. It is time to approach a literary agent. Send off query letters. Always enclose a self-addressed stamped envelope for the response. We do receive many such queries each week, and letters without the enclosure often end up in the waste basket. Always remember that it is often as difficult to find an agent as it is to find a publisher, and the more professional your approach, the more willing the agent will be to at least read your material.

Where You Find a Literary Agent
Two sources are *The Canadian Writer's Annual,* and *The Literary Market Place,* and there are other publishing directories and reference books. Ask your local librarian. A better and more likely way is an introduction through a fellow writer to his agent. The agent will know

her client would not introduce someone completely lacking talent. Ask a publisher. Many are willing to suggest an appropriate agent.

Why You Need a Literary Agent

You know you have written the great English-language work for children. You have received your mansucript back from New York, for reasons given above, and many others unopened, stamped "WE DO NOT ACCEPT UNSOLICITED MATERIAL," or "Interesting first page have your agent call," signed "the Editors." You have now blown a possible sale to New York. You may fare better in Canada, but don't expect a response for many months. Finally, you conclude you loathe writing the query letter to accompany your manuscript to the editor; you hate waiting in terror for the post person; you are far too nice to vet a contract. Besides, your nails are bitten to the bone, you have the personality of a slithy tove, your spouse is leaving, and your children hate you. If you don't get on with that new book running around in your head you will commit suicide. Get an agent.

Who the Best Agent Will Be for You

> "Curiouser and curiouser!" cried Alice (she was so much surprised, that for the moment she quite forgot how to speak good English).

Curious indeed, but it is a fact that few agents handle material for children. Begin your query letter to agents by stating that you write for children and asking if they are interested. Cordially ask if they do visit and know children's book editors throughout the world, and even more cordially ask how many writers of works for children they currently handle. Do they go to the annual Bologna Children's Book Fair? If you intend to make your career writing for children, it is understandably important to you whether or not children's writers are important to them. They will tell you.

Why is it agents do not seem much interested in the writer of works for children? Many think far too much effort is required for little financial reward. Far too many more editorial contacts to be made. Trips to Bologna are an extra expense in terms of both money and time. Advances are usually lower than those received for writers of adult material. "Curiouser and curiouser," but publishers too seem to think writing for children somehow rates less. As if shorter meant easier. Even more curious: agents often hear writers who have been unsuccessful placing an adult work say, "Well, I think I'll just write one for children. No problem." This, we all know, is not true. Shorter is rarely easier.

Fortunately, not all agents feel this way, nor publishers, nor most writers. Thus, your agent and others of like mind can only keep trying to bridge the gap between attitudes and current advances.

Alice may not believe in trying impossible things, but it needn't be true for you. There is use trying; one can believe in seemingly impossible things. Mad Hatters all.

P.S. Lewis Carroll had an agent.

8

Bringing Books to Children

Introduction

Once the publisher has completed the book, the job is not over. That book must be brought to the attention of the public, so that it will be purchased. This requires marketing people, reviewers, promotion people, librarians, and bookstore owners. Often books are not sold because the marketing strategies are unsuccessful or inappropriate. In this section the authors discuss their goals as those who bring books to children, and you may find clues in their articles that will help your writing or clarify your thoughts on how your books should be represented.

Some authors spend considerable time on the road in different cities being interviewed, speaking to children, to teachers and to parents, advertising their books. This is an arduous, time-consuming activity, but it does pay off. Other authors will use professional publicists, or those attached to the company. But very few books are successful without marketing. Bookstores can only stock so many books and so many copies of a book, and it is important for authors to recognize what bookstore owners look for. Librarians often determine the success of a book, and librarians purchase just like everyone else, from their budget. How to bring books to their attention is of importance to every author. Critics and reviewers who select from a number of books coming across their desks write about the ones that interest them, and their comments can be very useful for publicity.

This section reminds you as a writer to consider these important aspects of bringing books to children, since they may determine whether the children have your books to read.

Blowing Your Horn: The Author as Promoter

Kathy Lowinger

By its nature, writing is a solitary pursuit. Very few people write because they yearn to sit expectantly in a bookstore waiting to autograph books, or to try to capture the attention of sixty children in a drafty school gymnasium a thousand miles from home. Even the aggressive sound of the word "promotion" seems to be at odds with the notion of a quiet, contemplative art.

But writing a book is only one part of the process which will put it into a child's hand, and eventually into a child's heart. In order to read a book, the reader must know that the book exists. The purpose of promotion is to let people know about your book.

Promoting books for children in Canada is difficult and costly. The limited space available for reviews in newspapers or magazines for the general public means that many excellent books are never mentioned. Reviewing journals for professional teachers or librarians and academic journals are sources of information about books, but often the reviews appear months, or even years, after the book has been published. Because of the vast distances involved, sending an author on a media tour to television or radio stations across the country can be very expensive indeed. And, of course, air time is limited so the competition for the interviewer's attention can be fierce.

Effective promotion happens when the responsibility is shared by all the people involved in the process of producing a book.

The Publisher's Role

Ideally, 10 percent of the retail price of the book should be spent to promote it. If 5000 copies of your $10 book have been printed, in a perfect world $5000 would be available to promote it. Even if this sum were available for every book (and it almost never is), consider the cost of paying for display space for your book at a convention, the cost of preparing a catalogue, the cost of a poster, and the cost of a tour of a handful of cities. Promotional dollars, even when they are available, are quickly eaten up.

The publisher will prepare a catalogue listing your book, and will arrange to display it at conventions of booksellers, librarians and teachers. Depending on the publisher, the book's distributor may have sole or shared responsibility for a promotional catalogue. A poster or special bookmarks may be produced to publicize your book. The publisher may also make arrangements for you to go on a tour to talk about your book with the media.

The Bookseller's Role

The bookseller plays an important part in the process of promotion. He or she may prepare a newsletter for customers or a catalogue for mail orders. Readings and autographings may be part of regular programming. Most of these costs are met by the bookseller, so the competition for time and for the promotional budget of the store is great. Again, many good books may not be showcased.

The Teacher's and the Librarian's Role

Many teachers and librarians play an important role in promotion, because they want youngsters to read the books they provide. One of their most valuable promotional tools is the arrangement of visits by authors, because that personal contact is a superb way to encourage children to discover books and to begin to understand the creative process. Authors who enjoy working with children find that visits can be a good way to keep in contact with the interests of their young readers. Of course, readings can also represent a substantial source of income.

Libraries, bookstores and community centres are eligible for public readings funded by the Canada Council. These must be open to the public, well publicized and free of charge. Hosts of public readings are responsible for making the initial arrangements with both the author and the Council. The Canada Council pays the author fees and travel costs for public readings; the host must pay all other costs.

Some provincial governments fund school readings by authors. Most schools are responsible for paying all or part of the author's expenses, while the province pays all or part of the reading fee. Where provincial programmes do not exist or have been fully subscribed, host schools must pay both the author's fee and the author's expenses.

The Canadian Children's Book Centre's Role

The Centre was established in 1976 to promote the reading and writing of Canadian books for young people. The Centre offers a reference library, open to the public; courses on writing for children; special events including tours by authors; and biographies and bibliographies.

The Author's Role

What can you do to make sure that your book reaches the children for whom you have written it?

1. Assume that your publisher wishes to sell your book just as fervently as you do. After all, a massive investment of money and time is devoted to the production of every book. Approach promotion as a joint concern.
2. Think about the implications of promotion when you are negotiating your contract. Are there specific plans for the promotion of your book? What are the publisher's expectations of you? This is the time to talk about what you are and are not prepared to do to help promote your book. Some authors have family commitments which prevent them from embarking on long tours. Others are terrified of speaking in public. Still others simply do not wish to make any public appearances. It is important for you to have a clear, realistic idea of your responsibility, and the publisher's expectations.
3. Arm yourself with a promotional kit. Your publisher may develop a kit for you, but do not assume that this will happen. Your kit does not have to be expensive or elaborate. It can simply be a file folder. Stock it with several black and white photographs, some of them of you with children, and which you have permission to reproduce. A brief biography, which a prospective host can use for publicity, is useful to have on hand. Some authors have bookmarks printed, listing their books. These come in handy for autographing at schools.
4. If giving readings is going to be part of your career as a writer, plan at least two kinds of presentations: one for adult audiences and one for children. You may assume that you will always be asked to speak to children approximately the age of those for whom you write. You may be wrong! Legion are the authors of hard-hitting young adult fiction who have faced the sweet faces of a kindergarten class. A good host will avoid such mismatches, but they can happen. Have at least one alternative prepared.

    Most presentations are between forty minutes and one hour long. What you choose to present should suit your own style. Don't feel that you have to be an entertainer: children are interested in hearing you read and in talking to you about your own childhood, the inspirations for your work, and your work habits.

    Think about any props you may need. If you write historical

fiction, an old item can spark discussion. Many authors like to show versions of their work at different stages. Your props will accompany you when you travel, so they should not be elaborate, irreplaceable, too heavy to carry or too large to check on a bus or a plane.

5. Often the sale and autographing of books takes place at readings. Make sure your publisher knows your schedule so that books can be available in local stores. Be realistic: your publisher cannot deliver books without adequate warning. But if you know you will be travelling extensively, discuss book sales as soon as possible. Some authors carry books to sell themselves.

Authors are beseiged with scraps of paper, and even other people's books are thrust at them after most readings. Plan your approach. You may wish to sign one copy for the library, or a sheet which the teacher can photocopy for distribution. Let the host know how you wish to handle autographs when you are making arrangements for your visit.

6. Several organizations can help provide you with information and support. The Canadian Children's Book Centre welcomes questions from all writers, published and unpublished. Among its services is an annual workshop, Readings and Writing, for authors who are involved in giving readings. Membership in the Centre is $20.00.

The Canadian Society of Children's Authors, Illustrators and Performers (CANSCAIP) offers a wealth of services to writers, and works in many ways to promote your work. CANSCAIP is open to published and unpublished writers.

The Writers Union of Canada operates a year-round touring programme for authors throughout the country. It will also provide legal advice and information. To become a member, you must have at least one book published.

The Canadian Authors Association is one of the longest-established writers' associations in the country, providing information to its members and regular meetings in various parts of Canada.

If the idea of promoting your book is horrifying to you—did all this come from sitting at my desk and putting pen to paper?—remember that it can be a gratifying experience. You may find that it is lucrative. You will have the opportunity to see how youngsters react to your work. And you will meet people who have been moved by your words. They make the equation of writer-reader complete.

Reviewing Books for Children

Joan McGrath

Reviewing books for children and young adults is similar in many respects, but not identical, to reviewing adult materials. The great difference lies in the fact that the reader of your review is most unlikely to be a member of the audience for whom the book is intended, and may have no intention of reading even the most highly recommended titles.

The children's reviewer writes for the benefit of other adults, who will, perhaps, be guided by that reviewer's assessment of the material in question to select the item for inclusion in a child's private collection, or in a school, public or other library catering to children.

These readers require information and recommendations that will expedite their decision making. The reviewer must offer some guidance as to whether the book is well written, attractively presented, imaginative, informative, authoritative and/or accurate, depending upon the genre, and whether it is likely to prove controversial or offensive to any potential reader.

The person making the purchase knows the child's and/or the library's needs; the reviewer does not. Try not to tailor your recommendations too closely to the reactions of some particular child or group of children. Those youngsters may not be truly representative of the general public. What they like and enjoy may be far beyond the interest or ability range of a more typical audience of the same age group. Try to envision a generalized, average-reader group of about the age level indicated. Materials best suited to the needs or abilities of the extreme upper or lower reaches of that group should be identified as such.

It should not be necessary to mention the matter, but unfortunately it does require reiteration: read *all* of any item you accept for review. You owe it to the author of the book, and to the reader of your review, to be fully aware of the entire content. Reading the first few chapters and "the last bit" to get the flavour, just won't do.

What seems a dull title at the outset may, for all you know, take off into wonderland midway through. An apparently charming, innocuous work may at some point contain language or incident that would disturb or dismay a parent, teacher, librarian or young reader, and a good reviewer should serve notice on that score, providing the reader with all the relevant information required to make an informed selection. This is *not* to imply that "controversial" is necessarily "bad": merely that the reader of the review should be made aware of that particular aspect of the material before deciding to purchase.

It is probably a good idea to avoid reading other reviewers' comments on any title you will be reviewing yourself. You will not want to let some other person's assessment of a work colour your own reaction, whether favourably or not. All a reviewer has to offer is an honest personal evaluative opinion; but that opinion must be his or her own, based on the strengths or weaknesses of the original material, assessed at first hand, not on another reader's opinion of that material.

No conscientious reviewer would think of using jacket blurbs as sources of information. They are almost inevitably fulsome in their praises (after all, they're there to sell the book, not to criticize it), and quite frequently they are inaccurate regarding its content .

Don't be savage, and don't get off smart cracks at the expense of the material you review. It is inexpressibly painful to an author to see his or her work roughed up in print, and it just isn't necessary.

Never forget that even a book that doesn't send ecstatic readers to the moon took a whole lot of effort on somebody's part; and that effort should be at least respected, if not admired.

Besides, think how foolish you will feel (and look) if the rest of the world disagrees with you, and the title in question is hailed as a masterpiece and wins some major award. It *has* been known to happen, and not all that long ago or far away either . . .

Don't take cheap shots. If you can be both sensitive and amusing, great; but if one of the two has to go, hang on to sensitivity.

Don't, *don't* ever pretend to expertise you lack. *Someone* will come out of the woodwork to set you straight on Napoleonic military strategy, the mating habits of the Blue-footed Booby, Etruscan burial art, or any other esoteric subject you can think of, if you *dare* to wing it in that expert's treasured area of arcane knowledge.

Be your own fiercest editor, checking fact and figure, bearing always in mind that an army of know-it-alls is out there ready and eager to get you if you don't.

On the other hand, if you do have a claim to special expertise in a particular subject area, the reader of your review is entitled to know that such is the case. It will lend weight and authority to your opinions on the matter at hand if all relevant qualifications you may have are appended to the review.

Make notes as you go. You will know the sort of thing that is likely to prove essential in the body of your review, and that *must* be absolutely accurate if you intend to make any direct quotations: names, places and dates, stunningly apposite sentences or even passages that seem to encapsulate the spirit of the work, or that are just too funny, too touching or too something-or-other to be left out.

If you don't make these notes at first reading, you will very likely spend hours riffling back through the pages to find that perfect, elusive scrap you think you remember (and you may have misremembered what you think you read, at that).

Practice tends to make this specialized form of note-taking easier. You will learn to recognize at first encounter those items that you will want to use in your review; and it's not a bad idea to make rather more notes than you actually expect to require. It's a great labour- and patience-saving device in the long run.

Make your notes on standard three-by-five cards rather than in a notebook or on a regular-sized sheet of paper, especially if you are transcribing quotations for later use. Any particular note will be a lot easier to find if filed under topic headings such as Titles, Dates, Quotation regarding . . . and so on, than if you have to search almost as far into your own notes as into the original text to find the particular item you require. You may want to keep some of these cards on permanent file: for example, matters of continuing interest such as author's biographical information, lists of awards, titles in a series, etc.

A word about the merely mechanical aspects of reviewing. Do check your spelling, punctuation, etc. If you don't, someone else will have to do so, and you probably won't like the result. Always type. Nobody else thinks that your peculiar handwriting is amusing, or wants to spend time deciphering it. Always double-space, leaving nice big wide margins for the editor to scribble in. Think of it this way: do you want him or her to scribble on your lovely work? It's surprising how often these simple aids to good relations, that are likely to spare you irate phone calls and typos in the finished product, are neglected.

When making recommendations to purchase, don't be too gender-conscious. Certainly some types of material will have greater appeal to girls than to boys, and vice versa, but that hardly requires emphasis. In an era sensitive to the issue of sexism in children's materials, it is advisable to avoid pigeon-holing any title as being "just for boys" or "girls only."

Read around the title you are reviewing. Find any other titles by the same author, and titles by other authors on the same topic or in the same genre. You may wish to make comparisons between the item you are reviewing and the best in its field, or perhaps with the best seller in the field: two very different criteria.

Keep a record of your work. Photocopy your manuscript if possible. Occasionally there may be an editorial query as to the content or intent of the review as submitted. It will be next to impossible for you to remember exactly what you wrote, days or possibly weeks before, unless you can refer to a copy.

As with any sort of writing that is to be available to the public (i.e., that is not a diary, journal, or private correspondence, and don't be too sure about *them*, either), try to do your writing early enough to have time for it to "cool" before you send it off to its destination. It's amazing how your perceptions can alter in a day or two, when you've come off the boil and can reread your work with increased objectivity. You'll catch mistakes you might have let slip by in the heat of the moment; and you may have second thoughts about the tone or vehemence with which you have treated the subject.

Quite apart from these considerations, it's always wise to avoid last-minuting just in case something unforeseen (such as writer's block) prevents you from squeezing in under the wire. Deadlines are inelastic. You don't want your editor holding you responsible for an incipient ulcer, do you?

Keep copies of your reviews as published, if only to look back over the years and gloat about how you just get better and better. More seriously, should you have occasion to review more than one work by the same author, which is entirely probable in the relatively narrow confines of children's reviewing, it will be very useful to you to be able to look back at your earlier comments. Do you wish to contradict anything you said earlier? Perhaps you do; but for heaven's sake don't do it without being aware that you are doing so. The author will not have forgotten, even if you have.

You are offering a review, not just an opinion. That means that it will not do simply to say "It's great!" or "It's terrible!" and let it go at that. Provide some evidence for your comments, through example, comparison or quotation. Say what you mean, and mean what you say. You won't go far wrong.

To Pass On the Good News: Reviewing Books for Children

Tim Wynne-Jones

Put simply and unglamorously, a book reviewer's function is to announce the publication of a new book during the period when the book can be readily purchased (and not before or after), and to create interest in the book by expressing an opinion, one way or the other, as to its merit. Unless one is writing for a book-trade paper, reviewing a book before the publication date serves no useful function. Similarly, to review a book even a year after it has come out is to invoke the wrath of booksellers, who may not have the book in stock, and to frustrate shoppers.

Any attention from the press is good publicity, a book promoter will say, though this is cold comfort to the author. In truth, it can be said, I think, that a poor notice stimulates a reaction from those who like the book, assuming they feel strongly enough about it; and controversy, even in the mild form of gossip, spreads the word of the book's existence, inevitably creating interest in it. It is important, I believe, for the reviewer to see his role in this wider context as primarily a town crier and beyond that only one voice in a dialogue, an exchange of opinions. In the print media, generally speaking, the power of a reviewer to affect public taste can be nicely undermined by a snappy letter to the editor. The editorial page in a newspaper or magazine is read, typically, by a lot more readers than the reviews page, thus helping to redress the balance of power.

Any reviewer not too caught up in his own importance hopes for debate. I recall lambasting a popular children's author in the *Globe and Mail* and hoping, even as I wrote the column, that the writer's enormous fan club would rise up in a single voice with a clamorous, indignant riposte. That this did not happen disappointed me. (As an aside, I would suggest that any teacher or parent wishing to involve children not only with books and writing but with the whole process of news reporting, might make this a project: the regular scanning of the newspaper, discussion and, when necessary, the writing of letters to the editor. It is an exercise in critical evaluation, writing and democracy.)

It is to be hoped that a reviewer will aspire to some of the objectivity one expects of a literary critic, but *a reviewer is not a literary critic* for a number of reasons that I hope to touch on in this essay. In place of critical objectivity, then, one might hope from a reviewer for fairness and a distinct point of view. I do not believe a reviewer should attempt to mask his taste or personality in the vain attempt to be objective. The result will inevitably be wishy-washy and of little interest to anyone. Having a discernible taste in books is especially crucial to the writer whose reviews appear in a regular column. Readers should have the opportunity to gauge, over time, the columnist's particular interests and overview and thereby come to their own conclusions about the reviewed material regardless of what the columnist's opinion may be. This is an important point: regular readers will soon learn to adjust to an opinionated reviewer and, indeed, recognize, on occasion, that a book the reviewer loathes might be precisely the kind of book they enjoy!

On the other hand, a reviewer ought not to use a review column as a soapbox for hammering home some narrow principle, however preciously held it may be. Both these extremes are boring and no reviewer should be boring. An important part of a reviewer's job is to be read.

I am asked, from time to time, if there are any guides to reviewing children's books. There are none, nor need there be. For there are great and lively reviews published weekly. Any novice intending to review books who has not, from time to time, perused the *Times Literary Supplement* and the *New York Review of Books,* to name but two, is being presumptuous. And one had better do this homework *before* one starts reviewing in any regular capacity. It is sometimes difficult to do once one is in the business oneself! Read well-written reviews not for content or for the reviewer's opinions, but for *structure* and for *rhythm*.

Establishing a personal point of view over time is particularly relevant in the reviewing of children's books, where a wide variety of value systems come into play. I am a writer with a background in the visual arts. Therefore, my own criterion in reviewing a book is, for the most part, literary and esthetic. I do not claim any expertise in children, their literary needs or their psychology, beyond having once been a child and having three of my own. There are those, obviously, who think of children's books quite differently than I do: who review a children's book for its educational, instructive value, for instance; or the book's usefulness in the class as back-up material for curriculum; its moral implications or sociological value in addressing issues and "isms" of the day; the book's value "for the consumer dollar;" or its tonic appeal as a tool of bibliotherapy. In the focus a reviewer might take, the world of children's books differs sharply from the world of adult literature and the children's book reviewer's job varies accordingly. This is readily seen in the context in which a review appears. Compare a review from a trade magazine with a review of the same book in an educational or library journal, a church quarterly or the Christmas issue of a women's magazine.

A profile of my potential audience was drawn for me when I first took on my column at the *Globe and Mail*. They were newspaper readers of no particular stripe, dipping here, alighting there, who just might read my column if it caught their fancy. In other words, I was not expected to write only for the publishing industry or librarians or even parents, but for the casual reader. It was expected that I be informative but also entertaining. But not entertaining at the expense of the book. A book review should never be an excuse for merely showing off one's wit or erudition. One must be wary of targetting one's intended readership. In the end writing for yourself is the best policy in any kind of writing.

I hope a few children read my reviews, but I do not write with them in mind as my audience. This is, frankly, ironic, if not weird— and one of the ongoing criticisms of the whole process of reviewing children's books. If I write to a consumer it is to one who will buy books for children, but for the most part I am writing *about* books not selling them. I write out of the child I was, who is alive in me still, and the adult I am, who presumably shares much of the same taste as his former self but may just have a better sense of the context in which the book exists. I *never* pretend to know what children like and adamantly believe that any adult who poses as an "expert" on children's taste is a fraud of the worst kind. *Children simply do not have uniform tastes and it is impertinent to think so.* I think that a review written for children might best be written by a child—with some inspired adult guidance to avoid the, "it's an okay book, I guess," syndrome common in such reviews.

Reviewers have varying degrees of autonomy. In most cases a newspaper or magazine will insist on certain stylistic parameters—one might be expected to recommend purchase of the book, for example— but otherwise, a reviewer is only constrained by the book(s) he is handed and the space available to review them in.

In my own case, the choice of what I review is entirely my own, a responsibility for which I am generally thankful although I sometimes find it onerous. Many concerns, far from literary, come into play in choosing books to review. There are political considerations: I am committed to the growth of an indigenous publishing industry in this country and openly promote Canadian books over works from the United States or Great Britain. I do not pretend to like every Canadian book I review, but we are at a stage in this country where lively criticism is infinitely more valuable than clapping ourselves on the back at how clever we are to be publishing books at all! This was the state of things only a very few years ago; it is time to move on. I also feel I have a mandate to review work from both small and large presses and from regional as well as mainstream publishers. I try to balance my coverage of picture-books and works of longer fiction and I also try to balance my particular penchant for fiction with coverage of non-fiction titles. In young adult novels I try to represent works of both realism and fantasy.

While a new author of promise is a thrill to discover, I try always to review new works by prominent authors, as a matter of respect, even when I find the work indifferent. It is unfair, as the writer in the "middle of the list" is the one most likely to be passed over in this regard, but one attempts to make up for this in the long run. If I have condemned a work by an author on one occasion, I will not go out of my way to do it again, for, as I have told writers whose books I have not liked or simply overlooked, time is long. One bad review is unlikely to kill a book let alone a writer. Having said that, however, as an exponent of Canadian culture, I am sometimes painfully aware of pulling my punches in reviewing. The writing community in this country is very small and incestuous; a fact even truer of the children's book community. We cannot support anything like a distinct critical community, though I am sure one will grow as does the industry. (It has been said that the eminent children's book critic, Sheila Egoff, has made a point of not getting to know children's writers so as not to compromise her critical standards. If this is the case, it is a noble exception to the situation in this country.) In the meantime, many reviewers will come from the ranks of published authors. It is worth remarking that this is not as major a conflict of interest as it may seem to some. It has always been thus with poets. As one poet told me: "If we didn't review each other, who would?" If only children's writers had as thick skins as poets!

The single greatest constraint on the reviewer is limited space. I have constantly a line-up of far more books worth reviewing than I will ever get to. And then, when one does review a book, there is the problem of how much one can meaningfully say about it. Space is seldom a problem when a book is either wonderful or dreadful, but it is inevitably frustrating to review a book when one feels there are niggling things wrong with it, or subtle things *right* with it, for that matter. A book reviewer seldom has the literary critic's luxury of time or column inches to consider and explore minutiae in a book. I recall with some regret writing a positive review of a sequel by a prominent author and then receiving several phone calls and letters from respected peers who thought the book was a facile waste of time, whipped off for the Christmas market, and not nearly as good or original as its predecessor. What rankled was that I fundamentally agreed with these sentiments, but in reading the book I had been struck most strongly by its readability—by the author's facility of style—and it was this feature which had dominated my review. When one has little space, one must sometimes choose one facet of the book to talk about, at the expense of a thoroughly rounded evaluation. I do not know a reviewer who doesn't wish it were possible to write some reviews over again! Sometimes the value of a book does not dawn on one for many months, even years, after it is published. And equally, though one tries to stay clear of it, a reviewer is capable of getting caught up by the hype of a book's promotion or its superficial charm. It's an occupational hazard.

One's first priority as a book reviewer, however, is simply to love books. If there is one constant in my reviewing, I would hope that it is enthusiasm for what books can be when an author writes out of personal conviction, to tell us a story of who we are, pimples and all. I don't want to hear homilies dressed up to look like fiction. I don't want to hear thinly disguised classroom hectoring. I don't want to see television trends translated into print. What I look for is a story. And I listen for a voice longing to catch the ear. As a reviewer, I then try to respond in kind. To pass on the good news.

The Role of the Library

Marge Kelley

As a librarian, I look at books, I handle books, I read books, and I read about books. I do several of the above before I buy books.

The benefits of reading a book before purchasing are obvious. It is the one way to make a fully-informed evaluation of the merits of a particular book, and to consider its place in a particular library collection. It is equally obvious that it is not possible to read all the books that are being considered for purchase. That is why I browse in bookstores. I need to handle a book, to hold it, to open the pages, see the print size, the layout, the graphic design, the illustrations. I am very fortunate to live within reach of the Children's Book Store in Toronto, and I know that I can go there to see all the important new titles as they are available. I can also attend publishers' displays at conferences. However, I still need to take further steps to cover the output of new publications, and so I depend on my Board of Education's selection services and the reading of catalogues and reviews. My Board, among others, holds regular review meetings, and displays new materials for ordering purposes. I read publishers' catalogues to check off titles that I want to watch for, and I read reviews. I do not subscribe to a list of standard reviewing periodicals because of cost, but I never miss the reviews in the local newspapers or those in *Quill and Quire*, the monthly publication of the Canadian book trade. The bimonthly insert, *Books for Young People*, is particularly valuable. In addition to the above, I pay attention to wholesalers' catalogues when I know that there has been a selection process preceding the catalogue listing.

All of the above are part of the library selection process and part of my professional responsibility. They take time, but I am the organizer of that time, often outside of school hours. For that reason, and because my work day is fully committed to the library users, I do not accept publishers' calls or representatives in the school. I accept the responsibility for finding out about their products.

I take this responsibility of selection seriously, looking for different qualities in different kinds of books. In a novel, I want a well-written imaginative story, one that will hold my interest and that of the children to whom I will recommend it. For picture-books, the illustrations must complement the text to make a united whole. Non-fiction books must be accurate, the information must be well selected and presented, and the book must look like a book in which the information is readily accessible. And of course every book must be free of stereotypes and racial or ethnic bias.

As well as those general criteria, there are particular concerns in selecting children's books. One is that of knowing children's interests and matching those interests to books which the child can handle intellectually. For example, my dinosaur collection contains more than enough books for older children, who seldom use it, and not nearly enough for the under-eights, who are passionately interested in the topic. Writing informational books for young children without watering down the subject matter to meaningless generalities is a challenge to any writer. Current interests must be accommodated also. *On Your Mark, Get Set* by Paulette Bourgeois (Kids Can Press, 1987), a book about the Olympics, had to be in the library prior to and during the Calgary Games.

A new book on a subject hitherto not included in the children's collection receives special attention. Claire Mackay's *Pay Cheques and Picket Lines* (Kids Can Press, 1987) is the first book about labour unions and strikes written for young people. A new title which can replace outdated material is considered carefully: for example, *Parliament: Canada's Democracy & How it Works* by Maureen McTeer (Random House, 1987).

Comparative evaluation is another way of judging a new publication. A new title by a previously published author will be compared to the author's previous work. A new title on a familiar theme will be compared to previous publications on the same theme. A junior novel set during the Great Depression will have to have a hero or heroine as interesting as Booky in order to win a readership. (*That Scatterbrain Booky* by Bernice Thurman Hunter, Scholastic-Tab, 1981.) New writers must be aware of the particular field in which they are writing and have a good knowledge of the titles to which their work will inevitably be compared.

The school librarian, in particular, must be constantly looking for books to support the school curriculum. This involves knowing not just what is being taught, but the methods which are being used. It is a simple matter to look at *The Amazing Apple Book*, by Paulette Bourgeois (Kids Can Press, 1987) and see its use by the kindergarten teachers at the time of the annual trip to the apple orchard. It's more difficult to recommend a novel suitable for novel study, or to select a group of novels for a theme study. A thorough knowledge of the way in which teachers teach beginning reading is necessary to select picture-books in which patterning, predictability, and concept development occur. School librarians and teachers working together in the mode of *Partners in Action* (Ontario Ministry of Education, 1982), or in the co-operative planning teaching model, often share the responsibility of selecting materials. It is the librarian, however, who has the knowledge of the library collection as a totality, its strengths and weaknesses, along with a knowledge of all the library users. It is the librarian who uses this knowledge to develop the library collection to meet the needs of those users. Thus at different times, the librarian may be looking for books in languages other than English, books about ethnic minorities and customs, new books about various countries, and stories portraying non-traditional family patterns.

All of the effort which goes into the selection of books for a library is lost if the clients don't use the materials. Thus we always keep in mind what children want from the library. Often, unfortunately, it's what you haven't got—the book that hasn't even been written yet. Then the librarian's skills at suggesting acceptable substitutes come into play. I find it much easier to meet user needs in fiction than in non-fiction. Children often ask about "good books," and the introduction of a book by a teacher or librarian will keep the book moving for weeks. It's a different matter when they need an informational book for an assignment or a project. Then they become very specific. The ideal book would be at their reading level, would be relatively short, would have lots of pictures, graphs, tables and maps, would have lots of short paragraphs with bold type headings, and would cover exactly the things they want or are required to find out and nothing more! No one perfect book exists to meet all of this, so it becomes a matter of teaching them to select from several, to extract information from more than one source, and to cope with the inevitable lack of information on one or more aspects of the topic. The most important aspect of books of information for young children—the most difficult books to write—is that they look like books of information and not like storybooks. The young researcher (and many older ones) does not yet have the skills to extract facts buried in a lengthy narrative. They will quickly reject such a book with the remark, "No, that's a story book; I want information."

Keeping library users aware of new materials is an important item in library programming. Librarians traditionally use reading aloud, storytelling, book talks, displays and author visits as means of doing this. Author visits are a splendid way of promoting books, but money to provide them is often unavailable in the school budget. Promotional material is extremely valuable, but all too often the posters of new books aren't distributed to schools. I used to think it was greed that caused conference-goers to stuff their shopping bags with free posters. Now I find myself doing it with programming and book promotion uppermost in my mind.

One very important source of information and promotional material about Canadian books is the Canadian Children's Book Centre (229 College St., Toronto M5T 1R4). Their publications provide information about books and authors, and their sponsorship of the annual Children's Book Festival in November provides a Canada-wide focus for special events related to Canadian books and authors.

The existence of the Canadian Children's Book Centre since 1976 is certainly one of the reasons that Canadian books for children and young people have come of age in recent years. It is no longer necessary to deal with Canadian books using "special" evaluative criteria. I recall review meetings of the past when reviewers would tell all the weaknesses of a particular book and then end up by saying, "But it is Canadian," as if to say that we had a duty to select it in spite of its shortcomings. Today our Canadian authors and publishers are well enough recognized that their Canadianism does not need to be pointed out.

Canadian authors writing good books for children and young people will see their work marketed and read throughout the English-speaking world, and will be compared to writers of other countries. It is satisfying to know that when I select Canadian titles from among the hundreds that I consider, I will be offering in full confidence, the best material to my young readers.

The Role of the Bookstore

Judy Sarick

What does a prospective author or illustrator of children's books need to know about bookstores?

People I meet for the first time often say, "Oh, you have a book store! How nice it must be to sit and read all day!" Even customers in the store who see the 20 000 titles we stock sometimes express surprise that I have not read every one of them. Before any one of those thousands of books is displayed for sale, a lot of work must be done.

Buying Books

The publishing industry in Canada, like the clothing industry, has two seasons: fall and spring. Twice a year a sales representative, with her publisher's catalogues advertising their new titles, comes to visit the book buyer and presents (a trade euphemism for sell) all the new books. In Canada, book buying is possibly more complicated than in any other country. The United States, Britain, Canada, Australia, and any other country publishing in English want to sell their books here. If a book is simultaneously published in the U.S. and the U.K., these publishers decide between themselves who will have the Canadian rights. In the past these rights went to the country where the author lived. Now some authors are insisting on open rights for Canada. So, we now also have to decide which edition is the right one for our marketplace. The American editions have a look and binding that is more acceptable here, but usually they are more expensive than the British editions.

As a book buyer I must decide whether or not I like a book, if I feel it will sell in my store, and how many copies I want to start with. The sales rep, of course, wants me to choose every title she presents and to buy in large quantities. Sales reps must have thick skins to survive in a job in which most customers will take only a small percentage of their list. A good rep knows the buyer and her store and will not push her into taking more titles or copies than meet a reasonable sales expectation.

Before I buy a book, I like to see a finished copy or folded and gathered sheets, especially when it is a picture-book. Advertising in the publishers' catalogues is precisely that—advertising. I can choose a non-fiction title from a description of the content and format, but many novels are described as "heart-warming," so unless I have read earlier novels by an author or I trust the judgement of the rep, I pass over a novel and order it later if it gets good reviews. Then, of course, I run the risk of not being able to get the book when it is in demand. Often I will just take an educated guess, being cautious with the quantity. Buying an unseen title from a publisher I know is less of a risk.

How do I tell that a book is one I want to stock? Fortunately, our store is large enough for me to be able to buy any book I like. My taste in children's books has been developed throughout my lifetime: as a child reader and borrower from "Boys and Girls House" of the Toronto Public Library, as a page and reader at Forest Hill Junior High, as an honours Philosophy and then Librarianship student at the University of Toronto, as a children's librarian in a public library, as a teacher of children's literature at several Faculties of Education, as a school librarian and library consultant, as a reader to and with my own children, their friends and relations, and finally as a buyer and seller of books in The Children's Book Store for the past fourteen years. I have learned to look at a book from many points of view. The best ones are those that can stand up to that scrutiny—in other words, books that contain many levels of meaning, books which a child will reread at different ages and still discover something new. Not all the books I buy meet these criteria, but I do want a novel to tell a story and the information in a work of non-fiction to be accurate and well presented. I watch for a hundred other details that are second nature to me.

Displaying Books

After I have made the semi-annual decision about which titles to buy from twenty-five sales reps for over a hundred publishers with over a thousand titles, that information, along with our classification, must be entered into our computer data base. When the books arrive they must be unpacked, checked against my original order, labelled for price and section, and put on display for sale. In our store we have a system for displaying all new books with their front covers showing. How attractive the cover is and how well it represents the content is very important. Most people do "judge a book by its cover."

How long a book remains on display at the front of the store depends upon a number of factors. The first is the time of year and how many books are being published. In the Christmas season many beautiful books vie for space. In January few new books are published so a book can stay on display longer, but far fewer books are sold. If a book is selling well it is left on display. For example, *How to Make Pop-Ups* was on display all through the fall of 1987 and well into the spring of 1988. Throughout the year we also create displays of books on topics of current interest, such as spring, the Olympics, books nominated for, or receiving, awards, Reading Rainbow titles, etc.

Within each section of the store—picture-books, science, traditional stories, fiction, social studies, jokes and riddles, etc.—we also rotate the titles on face-out display. A well-done display is one of the most effective ways of selling a book.

Selling Books

When adult customers buy books for children they are usually far less confident than when they buy for themselves or for another adult, and therefore, they expect far more advice from the bookstore staff. "What is the best book for a very bright six-year-old?" "What do you have for my nephew in Saskatoon? He's eight, no maybe he's nine. You sold me beautiful books last year." "I need the most beautiful baby book for the fifth child in this family." "Who is the most popular author for ten-year-olds?" Every day we are asked such questions and many more. Many customers choose their own books from our vast selection and occasionally check to see if we think they have made appropriate choices. Others, especially at Christmastime when they are buying for children they know only slightly, are anxious for as much sales help as we can give them.

Some of my staff have a background in children's literature. They train the others to look more critically at the books we have selected to sell and to read more widely. Every one of the staff has his or her favourites, either from their childhood or from their reading in the store, and these are the books that they find the easiest to sell. Many of our customers are children and if left to their own devices by the adult who brought them, they are best able to choose the books that will satisfy their own needs. Children who come to the store in class groups sell each other the books they love best.

Author appearances in the store help to sell many more books if the author is well known and loved or has a large family and circle of friends. No one will come to the store to see an author who is not known. Many authors and entertainers (we also sell records) make appearances in the store, but never just to sign autographs. A child needs to have some involvement with the creator of the book or record in order to deepen her understanding. A signed book as a collectable object is an adult concept.

When authors come to the store they must be comfortable reading, answering questions, telling how they became writers, etc., thereby drawing the children into their creative process. The adults who have brought the children are also fascinated by this process and become more interested in buying those books and sharing them with their children.

Much of the work that goes on in a bookstore is not obvious from the sales floor. While one or two staff members are actually selling books to retail customers, others are receiving, reordering, shelving, labelling, paying bills, working on catalogues, returning books that haven't sold, entering data on the computers, ordering supplies, making signs for displays, straightening their sections, dusting, and performing any of the other ongoing tasks that must be done to make a business a success.

Reordering Books

In a bookstore there is a constant struggle between having too many books and too few books. Decisions are constantly being made about which books to keep in stock. Some books must always be in—*Charlotte's Web, Alligator Pie, The Hobbit, Madeline* and perhaps another thousand titles. As the new books come in and sell out we must decide whether they sold quickly enough for us to reorder or if the book is one we wish to continue to sell. Even with a store the size of ours (650 m²) we cannot continue to stock every book that we initially ordered. These decisions are easy to make with regard to mediocre books that sell slowly. One of the most difficult decisions is to drop a book I like because it no longer sells. Our computer system (Wordstock) makes it much easier to follow the sales history of a book and return it at the appropriate time or reorder with speed if sales of a book take off.

Canada has many "children's only" bookstores as well as many general bookstores with extensive children's book departments. Each one has its own style and flavour and method of doing business. We must all deal with what is presented to us by the publishers and try to run a viable business selling "low ticket" items at a limited profit margin. The bookseller who survives the complexities of the Canadian publishing industry and marketplace must be both astute and devoted to the idea of bookselling.

Biographies

Mary Blakeslee   Mary Blakeslee began writing in 1980 while she was a media consultant with the Manitoba Board of Education. When her first children's book was published, *It's Tough to be a Kid* (Scholastic, 1982), she started to write full time. Several books have followed, including *Halfbacks Don't Wear Pearls* (Scholastic, 1986), *Carnival* (Overlea House, 1987), *Will to Win* (Overlea House, 1988), *Chocolate Pie for Breakfast* (Avon, 1988), *Rodeo Rescue* (Overlea House, 1988) and *Museum Mayhem* (Overlea House, 1988). Mary lives in Calgary with her husband, Clem, where she enjoys gourmet cooking and photography when she isn't writing.

Jean Booker   Jean Booker was born and educated in England where she spent much of her time as an adolescent writing to pen-pals around the world. Her correspondence with a pen-pal in Montreal lasted for ten years—until, in 1955, she emigrated in order to visit her friend. She spent a year in Montreal, then moved to Toronto where she married. Jean and her husband have two daughters.

In 1975 Jean attended a creative writing class; she had her first short story published a year later. Since then she has had numerous short stories published in school anthologies, the *Canadian Children's Annual* and various magazines. She has also had one novel published, *Mystery House* (Overlea House, 1987).

David Booth   David Booth is a professor of children's literature at the Faculty of Education, University of Toronto. As well, he is a popular international speaker and an author of many books for both children and teachers.

Marion Crook   Born in Westminster, British Columbia, Marion Crook grew up in Surrey with three sisters, two brothers and a cousin. She graduated from Seattle University in 1963 with a B.Sc. in Nursing and then worked as a community health nurse in the Cariboo country of B.C. until 1982. Marion's writing has included non-fiction, short stories, drama and a novel series for young adults, the *Susan George Mysteries* (Overlea House). Her most recent works include "The Capitalist" on *Vanishing Point* (CBC, March 13, 1987), *Teenagers Talk About Suicide* (NC Press, 1988), *Hidden Gold Mystery* (Overlea House, 1987) and *Crosscurrents* (Overlea House, Fall 1988).

In 1964, Marion married Bill Crook in Williams Lake, B.C. She has raised three children and a step-daughter and now lives in New Westminister where she writes full time, teaches occasionally and enjoys the theatre and the arts.

Beatrice Culleton   Beatrice Culleton was born in St. Boniface, Manitoba, as the youngest of four children. She did not begin writing until the age of thirty-one, when a second suicide in her family led her to writing as a way of dealing with what had happened. This resulted in the publication of her first novel, *In Search of April Raintree* (Pemmican Publications, 1983). At this time she also became the manager/editor of Pemmican and developed its programme of publishing books of contemporary and traditional Native stories for children. Beatrice now lives and writes in Toronto.

Diane Dawber   Born in Belleville, Ontario, Diane Dawber trained as a teacher at Peterborough's Teachers' College, and received her B.A. and M.Ed. from Queen's University. She is also a graduate of the Banff Centre. Diane has had numerous poems and articles published as well as two books: *Cankerville* (Borealis Press, 1984) and *Oatmeal Mittens* (Borealis Press, 1987). She has received the Federation of Women Teachers' Associations of Ontario Writer's Award twice (1984 and 1987) for her writing. Diane is a teacher/librarian with the Lennox and Addington Board of Education and lives with her husband and two sons near Amherstview, Ontario.

David Dueck   In 1973, David and Toni Dueck incorporated Dueck Films and set out as a team to create a Canadian film company capable of producing high quality productions for the family entertainment market. Films they have produced include *St. Laurent Speaks* (1973), *Menno's Reins* (1975), *And When They Shall Ask* (1983) and *Families* (1986), as well as numerous other films, commercials and audio-visual productions for advertising agencies and clients such as the Canadian National Institute for the Blind. Films produced by Dueck Films have won numerous awards, including the White Owl Award, the Silver Screen Award from the Chicago Industrial Film Festival, and have been finalists in the Canadian Film and Television Association Awards.

Sylvia Funston   Sylvia Funston is the editor of *OWL* magazine, an international science and nature magazine for children, published in Canada, the United States, Britain, France and Italy. She has also been a consultant on several cross-media projects of the Young Naturalist Foundation, the non-profit publisher of *OWL* magazine, in particular the CBC/PBS award-winning OWL/TV series. Sylvia's background in photography and design enhances her versatility as a children's communications specialist and makes her much in demand as a lecturer and workshop leader within the industry. She has been given the Distinguished Achievement Award for Excellence in Educational Journalism by the Educational Press Association of America (EDPRESS) nine times.

Laszlo Gal   Laszlo Gal was born and raised in Budapest where he was educated in the dramatic arts and at the Superior School of Pedagogy from which he graduated as an art teacher in 1954. In 1956, he came to Canada and worked as a graphic designer at the CBC. He went to work as an illustrator for Arnoldo Mondadori in Verona, Italy in 1965. In 1969 he returned to Canada where he worked in graphic design and eventually as an illustrator of children's books. Books he has illustrated include *The Twelve Dancing Princesses* (Methuen, 1979), which won the Canada Council Award and the Canadian Library Association Amelia Frances Howard-Gibbon Award, *Willowmaiden* (Dial Books) and *Raven Creator of the World* (McClelland & Stewart).

Ted Harrison   Born in the mining village of Wingate, County Durham, England, in 1926, Ted Harrison received his education in art and an Art Teacher's Diploma. He immigrated to Canada with his wife and son in 1967, and later earned his B.Ed. at the University of Alberta. Ted has served with the British Army Intelligence Corps in India, Egypt, Uganda, and Somaliland, and taught in England, Malaysia, New Zealand and Canada. He has received awards for his design and illustration work, and has been a member of the Order of Canada since 1987.

Ted's published works include *Children of the Yukon* (Tundra Books), *The Lost Horizon* (Merrit Publishing) and the forthcoming *The Blue Raven* (Macmillan), all written and illustrated by him. He has illustrated two Robert Service poems, "The Cremation of Sam McGee" and "The Shooting of Dan McGrew," (Kids Can Press). Ted also designed the Yukon Pavilion for Expo '86. He currently lives in Whitehorse, in the Yukon.

Monica Hughes   Monica Hughes was born in England and spent her early years in Egypt. She was educated in England and Scotland. When she moved to Canada in 1952, she worked for the National Research Council. She now lives in Edmonton with her husband and four children. Although Monica always dreamed of being a writer, it was not until 1971 that she began to write seriously for young people. She had twenty novels published between 1974 and 1987, most of which were science fiction, as well as many short stories. Monica has won numerous awards, including the Vicky Metcalf Award for a body of work in 1981, the Alberta Culture Writing-for-Young-People Competition for *Hunter in the Dark* (Irwin, 1982), the Canada Council Prize for Children's Literature twice for *The Guardian of Isis* (Hamish Hamilton, 1981) and *Hunter in the Dark* and the Writers Guild of Alberta R. Ross Annett Award for Children's Literature for *Hunter in the Dark, Space Trap* (McRae Books, 1983) and *Blaine's Way* (Irwin, 1986).

Bernice Thurman Hunter   Born and educated in Toronto, Bernice Thurman Hunter has been interested in writing since childhood. As a young mother she composed stories for her own children with them as the protagonists. But she did not begin to publish until she was fifty. Her first novel, *That Scatterbrain Booky* (Scholastic-Tab), won the IODE Book Award and was short-listed for the Toronto Book Award in 1981. She has published several novels since then, as well as numerous articles and short stories, including two more Booky novels, *A Place for Margaret,* and *Margaret on Her Way* (both from Scholastic-Tab). Her strength as a writer lies in her ability to bring childhood memories vividly to life. Her books are becoming increasingly popular, and she is in constant demand as a guest speaker across Canada.

Valerie Hussey   Valerie Hussey graduated from the State University of New York, Buffalo, in 1972 with degrees in English literature and education. She then began to work in educational publishing, working for Macmillan and Harcourt Brace Jovanovich, in New York. In 1978, Valerie moved to Canada and became involved with Kids Can Press in 1979, assuming control of the company in 1981. She is now co-owner of Kids Can Press as well as publisher and president. Valerie is also Chairperson of the Board of Directors of The Canadian Children's Book Centre and of Children's Literacy Toronto and sits on the Advisory Council of Theatre Direct and the Board of Directors of the Vermont Square Mother-Child Mother Goose Project.

Marge Kelley   Marge Kelley was born and raised in Nova Scotia where she trained to be a teacher. She has taught in Nova Scotia, Quebec and Ontario. After moving to Ontario, she went back to school to further her studies in education and library science. She also spent a year at the Institute of Education at the University of London in England. She has had a number of articles and books published about children's literature and school libraries. Marge lives in Toronto, where she is a teacher/librarian at Frankland Community School and a lecturer in school librarianship at the Faculty of Education, University of Toronto.

Joanne Kellock   When Joanne Kellock was a little girl, she spent many dark and stormy nights sitting close to her grandmother and listening to stories. There were stories of knights: green, red, white and black; tales of goblins, fairies, elves, witches and dragons; and best of all, the works of Lewis Carroll and the Brothers Grimm. Later she earned an Honours B.A. in English at the University of Alberta. She then travelled, lived and worked in England, did graduate work in publishing at Harvard/Radcliffe, and raised three children. She is now a literary agent living in Edmonton, where she spends many dark and stormy nights reading to her very young granddaughter.

Maryann Kovalski   Born and raised in New York City, Maryann Kovalski attended the School of Visual Arts where she studied animation and illustration. Upon graduation she worked for various magazines and newspapers. She later immigrated to Montreal. In 1977, she

and her husband moved to Toronto where she was given her first opportunity to illustrate a children's book: Allen Morgan's *Molly and
Mrs. Maloney* (Kids Can Press, 1982). Several books followed this one
including *Brenda and Edward* (Kids Can Press, 1984), both written and
illustrated by Maryann, *I'll Make You Small* (Douglas & McIntyre,
1986), and the forthcoming *Jingle Bells* (Kids Can Press, Fall 1988),
also written by Maryann. Maryann Kovalski still lives in Toronto, and
now finds that her professional life is wholly concerned with illustrating
and writing books for children.

Jean Little   Jean Little was born in Taiwan where her parents were
missionaries. The family returned to Canada when she was seven.
Despite impaired vision, Jean attended regular schools and graduated
from the University of Toronto. She was a teacher until 1962 when her
first novel, *Mine For Keeps,* was published and won the Little, Brown
Canadian Children's Book Award. Since then she has had twelve
novels, two books of poetry and an autobiography published, including
Listen for the Singing (Dutton, 1977), which won the Canada Council
Children's Literature Prize, and *Mama's Going to Buy You a Mocking
Bird* (1984), which won the Canadian Library Association Book of the
Year for Children Award and the Ruth Schwartz Children's Book
Award. In 1974, Jean was given the Vicky Metcalf Award for a body
of work. Jean writes full time now with the aid of a talking computer
and travels with her guide dog, Zephyr.

Celia Barker Lottridge   Celia Barker Lottridge has been a children's
librarian and elementary school teacher/librarian. She has a M.L.S.
from Columbia University and B.Ed. from the University of Toronto.
She was a buyer for the Children's Book Store in Toronto for eight
years and is now a consultant on children's literature for them. She
works as a storyteller in schools, conducts courses and workshops on
storytelling and writes for children. She is a founding member of the
Storytellers School of Toronto and of the Parent-Child Mother Goose
Program, which uses rhymes and stories. She also works through Inner
City Angels and has taught storytelling for the Haliburton School of
the Arts and the Saskatchewan School of the Arts. Her published
works include *Gerasim and the Lion* (Bright Star Books), *One Water-
melon Seed* (Oxford) and the forthcoming *The Name of the Tree*
(Groundwood).

Kathy Lowinger   Kathy Lowinger was educated at the University of Toronto and at the University of Cambridge. After completing studies in social anthropology, including a year-long field trip to Antigua, she worked for the Ontario Association for the Mentally Retarded. She worked with parents' groups across the province to help establish a wide variety of community services for people who have disabilities.

Kathy has been with The Canadian Children's Book Centre since 1984 as Executive Director. The Centre is a national, non-profit organization established in 1976 to promote the reading and writing of literature for young people. She is also a regular contributor to *School Libraries in Canada*.

Her interests include reading children's books, folk music and Spanish classical dancing. The job of executive director involves a great deal of travel; therefore, one of her interests has become being able to stay home on vacation.

Janet Lunn   Born and raised in the United States, Janet Lunn came to Canada in 1947 to attend grade thirteen in Ottawa. She stayed in Canada, was married in 1950 and raised five children. Her first published work was a history of Prince Edward County, *The County,* written with her husband, Richard, and published by the County in 1967. In 1968 her first children's novel, *Double Spell* (Peter Martin Associates) was published. It was followed by others, including *The Twelve Dancing Princesses* (Methuen, 1979), which won the IODE Book Award for 1979 and was chosen as one of the ten best children's books of that year by the Canadian Library Association; *The Root Cellar* (Lester & Orpen Dennys, 1981), winner of numerous honours including the Canadian Library Association Book of the Year for Children Award and *Booklist's* Reviewer's Choice; and *Shadow in Hawthorn Bay* (Lester & Orpen Dennys, 1986), winner of the Canada Council Children's Literature Prize and the National Chapter IODE Book Award. Janet continues to reside in Prince Edward County.

Claire Mackay   Claire Mackay was born and educated in Toronto. She has worked as a librarian, social worker and rehabilitation counsellor. In 1978 she began to write full time. Her books include *Mini-Bike Rescue* (1982), *One Proud Summer* (co-author Marsha Hewitt, Women's Press, 1981), *The Minerva Program* (James Lorimer & Co.,

1984) and *Pay Cheques and Picket Lines* (Kids Can Press, 1987). She has been awarded the Ruth Schwartz Children's Book Award (1982) and the Vicky Metcalf Award both for a body of work (1983) and for her short story, "Marvin & Me & The Flies" (illustrated by Maryann Kovalski) published in the Canadian Children's Annual, 1987 (Overlea House).

Eva Martin   Eva Martin was born in Woodstock, Ontario, but has spent most of her life in Toronto. As a child Eva was a voracious reader. She was educated as a librarian and she worked as a children's librarian at the Toronto Public Library where she took part in training sessions in storytelling, puppetry, mythology, epic literature, children's literature and book reviewing. These areas have been the focus of her work since then. Eva is the Co-ordinator of Services for the Scarborough Public Library Board, a position that allows her time to go into schools to tell stories and give talks on folklore. In 1984 she published *Canadian Fairy Tales* (Groundwood). Eva lives in Toronto in a one-hundred-year-old house where she indulges her passions for gardening, reading and cooking, and plays games with two cats who are really her alter egos.

Joan McGrath   Joan McGrath has worked in and for children's libraries since first becoming a page at age nine. When her three children were of school age, she attended Teachers' College and became a teacher/librarian, eventually working as a library consultant for the Toronto Board of Education. Since 1972 she has been a regular reviewer of both adults' and children's material, with reviews appearing in numerous publications, including *The Toronto Star, Quill & Quire, School Library Journal* and the *Canadian Book Review Annual*. Joan is the book review editor for *Reviewing Librarian* (Ontario Library Association). She is also an occasional lecturer on children's literature. Her articles and critical essays have appeared in various publications and anthologies, including regular columns in the *Toronto Star, Emergency Librarian* and *In Review*.

William H. Moore   Born and educated in England, Bill Moore served for seven years with the RAF before immigrating to Canada in

1946. He was supervisor of curriculum and instruction (English) at the Hamilton Board of Education at the time of his retirement in 1977. He has had a book, *Words That Taste Good* (Pembroke), stories, poems and plays published in Canada, the United States and England and was co-author of *Nobody in the Cast* (Academic) and *Poems Please* (Pembroke). Bill has also written and read stories and articles for the CBC.

sean o huigin   In 1969, sean o huigin became involved in the first Ontario Arts Council Artists in Schools programme and with the Inner City Angels, who run a similar programme. Throughout the 1970s and 1980s he has continued his work in schools in Canada, the United States and Great Britain. Since 1960, he has been involved in adult poetry readings and performance art. His latest poetry books for children include *Ghost Horse of the Mounties* (Black Moss Press, 1983), for which he won the Canada Council Children's Literature Prize, *I'll Belly Your Button in a Minute* (Black Moss Press, 1985) and *Pickles and the Dog Nappers* (Black Moss Press, 1986). sean divides his time between Canada and Ireland.

Stéphane Poulin   Encouraged by his father, Stéphane Poulin has been an avid artist since he was six years old. He began his professional career in 1983, after graduating from a graphic arts course at College Ahuntsic. Since then he has made videos and has illustrated many children's books, including *Have You Seen Josephine?* (Tundra, 1986), for which he received the Canada Council Children's Literature Prize. Stéphane has also received awards for his work from Communication-Jeunesse. His other works include *Les animaux en hiver, Teddy Rabbit,* and a series forthcoming from Annick Press in 1989. Stéphane lives and works in Montreal.

Ken Roberts   Ken Roberts is the author of *Crazy Ideas* (Groundwood, 1984), *Pop Bottles* (Groundwood, 1987), and *Hiccup Champion of the World* (Groundwood, 1988). He also co-authored a hit Vancouver play and is a CanPro award winner for children's television writing. Ken has performed across Canada as a storyteller. He writes only in his spare time; he spends his days as chief librarian of the Whitby Public Library in Whitby, Ontario.

Judy Sarick   Judy Sarick received a B.A. and a B.L.S. from the University of Toronto. She was a children's librarian and later became the school library consultant for the Etobicoke Board of Education. In 1972, she was the acting head of school libraries for the Toronto Board of Education. She established The Children's Book Store in Toronto in 1974 to provide children with the fine books which were available to them in libraries. Through the store Judy has initiated many innovative programmes, including class visits for school children, a children's literature course for parents and visits by authors, illustrators, story-tellers and musicians from around the world. In 1979, she received the Bookseller of the Year Award from the Book Publishers' Professional Association. As well as teaching children's literature at the University of Toronto and the University of Western Ontario, Judy has given workshops on children's literature for conferences and professional development days. She has also written reviews of children's books for the *Toronto Star*.

Stanley Skinner   Born in London, England, Stanley Skinner received his B.A. in English from the University of Saskatchewan. He has worked as an editor for *Farmers Weekly* magazine (London, England) and for Longmans Canada as an editor of educational materials; and has edited flight training manuals for the RCAF in Saskatoon, as well as working free-lance. His own works include *The Advertisement Book* (Doubleday, 1975), *The ABC's of Creative Writing* (Globe/Modern Curriculum Press, 1981) and *Only Novels: A Study of Genre in Fiction* (Globe/Modern Curriculum Press, Fall 1988). The latter two are co-authored with David Booth. Stan is also an instructor in book editing and writing as well as the co-ordinator of the book and magazine publishing programme at Centennial College, Scarborough, Ontario.

Barbara Smucker   Barbara Smucker's writing career began fifty years ago with short stories she wrote for the newspaper at the University of Kansas where she was a journalism student. She became a journalist, raised a family, and has worked as a bookseller, a teacher and a librarian. Her first novel, *Henry's Red Sea* (Herald Press), was published in 1955, and was followed by nine more. Her works include *Underground to Canada* (Clarke, Irwin, 1977), which won the All-Japan School Library Award (1983) and the Catholic Teachers' Association Award (West Germany, 1983), *Days of Terror* (Clarke, Irwin,

1979), which won the Canada Council Children's Literature Prize, *White Mist* (Irwin Publishing, 1985) and *Jacob's Little Girl* (Viking, 1987). Barbara has also been awarded an honorary Doctor of Letters from the University of Waterloo (1986) and the Vicky Metcalf Award for a body of work (1988).

Ted Staunton   Ted Staunton was born and educated in Toronto, and is a graduate of Victoria College and the Faculty of Education of the University of Toronto. He is a writer and musician who has been entertaining children and adults since 1979. Books he has published include *Puddleman, Taking Care of Crumley* and *Maggie and Me* (all from Kids Can Press). He created two solo shows for children, "Flat Note Follies" and "The Nicholas Pennyworth's Peanut Butter Predicament," which have been performed at schools, libraries and the Toronto International Children's Festival.

Ian Wallace   Ian Wallace was born in Niagara Falls and educated at the Ontario College of Art. He is a children's writer and illustrator. He received the 1985 Canadian Library Association Amelia Frances Howard-Gibbon Award and the 1984 IODE Book Award for *Chin Chiang and the Dragon's Dance* (Douglas & McIntyre, 1984). His other books include *Julie News* (Kids Can Press, 1974), *Sparrow's Song* (Penguin, 1986) and *Morgan the Magnificent* (Groundwood, 1987). He has met over 60 000 school children, and given workshops to thousands of librarians, teachers and writers.

Susan Wallace   Susan Wallace has been involved in curriculum development and teacher education for the past fifteen years: as a lecturer at the University of Toronto and as a consultant for the Peel Board of Education. Susan graduated from Hamilton Teachers' College and received her B.A. from McMaster University and her M.Ed. in curriculum design from Florida Atlantic State University. Susan has written extensively in the curriculum area. She is the senior author of the Primary Environmental Studies Series, a joint project of the Peel and Ottawa Boards of Education, and an advisor and contributing author to the Ministry of Ontario document, *Science Curriculum Ideas for Teachers.*

Susan's first stories for young children were published in a series of three books: *Family Shapes and Sizes, Family Ins and Outs* and *Family Ups and Downs* (Oxford University Press). She has recently completed a new easy-read novel, *The Raspberry Problem,* which won an award from the Federation of Women Teachers' Associations of Ontario (Overlea House, 1989).

Susan lives in Toronto and is the mother of two teenagers who claim that she gets all her story ideas from their lives.

Eric Wilson   At the age of twelve, Eric Wilson often stalked "suspicious-looking" people through the streets of Winnipeg, hoping to uncover a crime. Now, as a writer of mysteries, he creates crimes for his young sleuths, Tom and Liz Austen, to uncover. Eric's first novel, which has not been published, was written to show a bored grade eight class that books could be fun. He has continued to write books that are fast-paced and easy to read in order to entice reluctant readers. He has written fourteen books including *Murder on the Canadian* (Clarke Irwin/The Bodley Head, 1976), *Vampires of Ottawa* (Collins, 1984), *Summer of Discovery* (Collins, 1984), and most recently *Code Red at the Supermall* (Collins, 1988), set in the West Edmonton Mall. Eric lives in Victoria but travels widely to research his books and to visit schools to give readings.

Tim Wynne-Jones   Tim Wynne-Jones came to Canada from England when he was four years old. He has an honours B.A. from the University of Waterloo and an M.F.A. from York University. Tim has taught art at university, run his own graphic design firm, reviewed children's books for the *Globe and Mail,* and sung rock and roll. He has written radio plays, songs, an opera, six children's books and three adult novels. He has received several awards including the Seal First Novel Award for *Odd's End* (McClelland & Stewart, 1980), the IODE Book Award for *Zoom at Sea* (Douglas & McIntyre, 1983), and the ACTRA National Radio Award for *St. Anthony's Man* (1988). Tim's recent publications include *Fastyngange* (Lester & Orpen Dennys, 1988) and *Architect of the Moon* (Douglas & McIntyre, 1988).

Meguido Zola   Meguido Zola is the author of a number of children's books including *Only the Best* (Julia Macrae) and *By Hook or by Crook: My Autograph Book* (Tundra). His biographies of Canadians—for both children and adults—include studies of Jean Little, Dennis Lee, Farley Mowat, Monica Hughes, Douglas Tait, Sharon, Lois and Bram, Wayne Gretzky, and Terry Fox. Meguido lives in Vancouver where he is a professor of children's literature in the Faculty of Education, Simon Fraser University.

Bibliography

The Basics of Writing for Children, Published-Writer's Digest Publications, Cincinnati, 1987. A Writer's Digest Guide, Volume 5.

How to write and sell fiction, non-fiction and poetry for young people, from pre-schoolers to teenagers.

Book Talk: Occasional Writing on Literature and Children, Aidan Chambers, The Bodley Head, London, 1985.

In this collection of selected recent lectures, articles and essays, Aidan Chambers discusses literature, children, and the role of adults in bringing the former two together.

The Children's Picture Book: How to Write It, How to Sell It, Ellen E.M. Roberts, Writer's Digest Books, Cincinnati, 1986.

Roberts answers virtually every question asked by new children's authors: how to choose a subject, plot a story, use appropriate vocabulary, work with artists and sell your book to an editor.

The Children's Writer's Marketplace, S.F. Tomajczyk, Running Press, Philadephia, 1987.

The Children's Writer's Marketplace provides in-depth analysis of the major book publishers, top magazines, newspapers, and newsletters along with dozens of little-known outlets for such specialized projects as alphabet books, colouring books, TV scripts, how-to hobby guides, comic books, teen romances and preschool picture-books.

Gates of Excellence: On Reading and Writing Books for Children, Katherine Paterson, Lodestar Books/E.P. Dutton, New York, 1981.

Katherine Paterson shares what it means to be a reader and writer as she tells of the experiences that grew into books and also of the difficulties that surround writing.

How I Came to Be A Writer (revised and expanded edition), Phyllis Reynolds Naylor, Aladdin Books/MacMillan Publishing Company, New York, 1987.

This book is Phyllis Naylor's story about her stories, from her first work in kindergarten to her most recent books. Illustrated with photographs, and including samples of her earlier writings, this book demonstrates the inner workings of the writing process, from the spark of an idea to a book's actual publication.

How to Write a Children's Book and Get It Published, Barbara Seuling, Charles Scribner's Sons, New York, 1984.

Barbara Seuling, the author and illustrator of many books for children, worked for many years for major publishing houses as a children's book editor.

Lotus Seeds: Children, Pictures, and Books, Marcia Brown, Charles Scribner's Sons, New York, 1986.

These astute comments on books published for children during the past three decades include glimpses of Marcia Brown's early years as a teacher and a storyteller in the New York Public Library, and her observations about her own techniques and media, in addition to her experiences in bookmaking.

Modern Canadian Children's Books, Judith Saltman, Oxford University Press, Toronto, 1987.

This Canadian reference covers children's literature in Canada from 1975 to 1985, a decade of growth in writing for children.

Non-fiction for Children: How to Write It, How to Sell It, Ellen E.M. Roberts, Writer's Digest Books, Cincinnati, 1986.

A comprehensive guide to writing non-fiction books for five age groups—from toddlers to teenagers—and getting them published.

Part of the Pattern, Elaine Moss, The Bodley Head, London, 1986.

Elaine Moss takes the reader on a personal journey through the world of children's books, 1960 to 1985.

The Promise of Happiness: Value and Meaning in Children's Fiction, Fred Inglis, Cambridge University Press, Cambridge, 1981.

This book is a study of what is, in the author's opinion, the best children's fiction of the past hundred years and, at the same time, a study of the social values which that fiction celebrates and criticizes.

A Sense of Story: Essays on Contemporary Writers on Children, John Rowe Townsend, The Horn Book, Inc., Boston, 1971.

This book is an introduction to the work of nineteen leading English-language writers for children. It mixes American, British and Australian writers and includes brief biographical details and notes by the authors on themselves and their books.

Talent is Not Enough, Mollie Hunter, Harper & Row, New York, 1976.

In these public addresses, Mollie Hunter paints a vivid picture of her life as a writer and illuminates her novel settings with fascinating historical detail.

Touch Magic: Fantasy, Faerie and Folklore in the Literature of Childhood, Jane Yolen, Philomel Books, New York, 1981.

This collection of essays on the importance of fairytale and folklore points out the vital roles played by fantasy in the stimulation of the imagination and the acquisition of language, the essential tools of thought.

Treasures, The Canadian Children's Book Centre, Toronto, 1988.

Treasures is a catalogue of Canadian children's illustrators and can be seen as a measure of children's book art. The Centre, established in 1976 to promote the reading, writing and illustrating of Canadian children's books, has been a vital force in the growth of the industry during its decade of existence. In the mid-1970s an uncertain market, low press runs, and overwhelming competition from outside Canada made it impossible for Canadian publishing houses to produce more than a very few four-colour picture-books. In the mid-1980s Canadian children's books, many of them in full colour, are held in high esteem and sold around the world.

The Way to Write for Children, Joan Aiken, Elm Tree Books, London, 1980.

Joan Aiken offers advice on plot construction, character and the importance of inessential detail; discusses humour and fantasy and touches on the question of the moral message.

Writing for Children & Teenagers, Lee Wyndham/Revised by Arnold Madison, Writer's Digest Books, Cincinnati, 1968.

This classic book shares ideas for holding a young reader's attention, building characters and plots to a climax. It includes vocabulary lists based on age level, and much more.

Writing Short Stories for Young People, George Edward Stanley, Writer's Digest Books, Cincinnati, 1987.

This author of more than 100 published children's stories shows precisely what makes a successful short story for young people, spells out the requirements of each juvenile genre, and targets the needs of a variety of story markets.

Writing with Pictures: How to Write and Illustrate Children's Books, Uri Shulevitz, Watson-Guptill Publications, New York, 1985.

This informative guide details every aspect of creating a successful children's book—from telling the story, through planning the book and drawing the pictures, to preparing artwork for the printer.